SPIRALING INTO HEARING LOSS AND DEAFNESS

A Memoir of a Professors Decent into Hearing Loss

Juanita L. Malonson Holliman

To order additional copies of this book, contact:
Xlibris
844-714-8691
www.Xlibris.com
Orders@Xlibris.com

ISBN: Softcover   978-1-6641-6057-6
         Hardcover   978-1-6641-6058-3
         EBook   978-1-6641-6056-9

Library of Congress Control Number: 2021903918

Print information available on the last page

Rev. date: 04/27/2021

Imagine having been a professor for over twenty-five years and while concluding a lecture to over fifty health and wellness majors and eliciting questions from the class and motioning to one student who stood up in the back of the room and proceeded to ask a question, I could hear portions of his question, and then suddenly seeing the movements of his mouth, I could not hear what he was saying. And realizing that I had lost my hearing, I was frightened. I could not hear a word he uttered. The bottom of my world as a professor had suddenly come to an end. The thought of losing my hearing was almost unbearable.

There are thousands and thousands of deaf and hard of hearing people all over the world, and as the world turns, the world turns its back on the history and plight of those who are deaf or hard of hearing.

This is a book about the history and treatment of deaf and hard of hearing people around the world, the Americans with Disabilities Act, and Alexander Graham Bell's arguments on oralism versus sign language.

This book takes the reader on an eye-opening and absorbing epic educational journey. It will feed your hunger and thirst as you enjoy reading new knowledge about people with hearing disorders. The book is thought-provoking from beginning to end. The message in today's society to people who are hard of hearing or deaf is typically to "get a cochlear implant or a hearing aid and move on."

There is nothing written historically about African American deaf or hard of hearing slaves, prisoners in penal systems who are deaf or hard of hearing, or the sterilization and murder of deaf or hard of hearing people during the Third Reich in Germany.

There is an urgent need to share with the world the plight then and now about persons who, then and now, are deaf or hard of hearing. I hold a PhD in higher education and am a person who is currently experiencing the plights of not being able to hear clearly or understand what another person is saying, and it is frustrating and almost unbearable sometimes to the point of wanting to commit suicide. In addition, I also personally serve as a guest lecturer to health and wellness audiences.

This book has a worldwide appeal to all educators in every discipline there is, especially teachers and clinicians in health occupations, high schools, elementary schools, sociology, psychology, anatomy and physiology, physics, family services, and a host of other disciplines.

The world has begun to embrace deaf and hard of hearing cultures, as evidenced in countries such as China and other countries by opening Starbucks cafés specifically for deaf and hard of hearing individuals.

Perhaps offering this book in Starbucks cafés for sale to customers in stores around the world will help to spread knowledge and to boost the sales of the book around the world.

Sincerely,
Juanita L. Malonson, BSN, MSN, PhD
126 W Delaware Place. Apt100
Chicago, Ill. 60610
312-654-8243
Juanita holliman6@gmail.com

CONTENTS

PREFACE

This is a story of the wealth of information and facts uncovered about the deaf and hearing loss of individuals with this disability and the sudden loss of my hearing as a professor of nursing after thirty years of teaching and mentoring students.

As I searched for ways to aid me in my journey into the depth of hearing loss, I discovered information and facts about the plight of deaf and hard of hearing people that were beyond my wildest imagination. It is with this acquired wisdom that I wish to share what I uncovered with readers all over the world.

The story ideas for the book are created from the perspective of the historical and political treatment of people with hearing disabilities throughout the ages from thirty-five to forty-five thousand years ago to Hitler's anarchy and murderous reign of people who were deaf or hard of hearing.

I was unable to find books written that are similar and/or identical to the one I have written. The ones located focused on self-help topics, such as living with hearing loss and/or hearing loss for idiots.

I offer this book as a gift to patients, caregivers, scientists, scholars, and anyone who loves teaching and learning.

CHAPTER 1

Deafness and Hard of Hearing

To begin, several states have adopted into their laws the use of the terms "hard of hearing" as oppose to the term "hearing-impaired." This is the preferred term currently being used in today's literature.

"Deaf culture," as defined by Wikipedia, is the set of social beliefs, behaviors, art, literary traditions, history, values, and shared institutions of communities that are influenced by *deafness* and that use sign languages as the main means of communication. Many members take pride in their *deaf identity*.

According to the World Health Organization (2018), over 5 percent of the world's population—or 466 million people—have disabling hearing loss (432 million adults and thirty-four million children). It is estimated that by 2050, over nine hundred million people—or one in every ten people—will have disabling hearing loss. Disabling hearing loss refers to hearing loss greater than 40 decibels (dB) in the better hearing ear in adults and a hearing loss greater than 30 dB in the better hearing ear in children.

The majority of people with disabling hearing loss live in low- and middle-income countries. Approximately one-third of people over sixty-five years of age are affected by disabling hearing loss. The prevalence in this age group is greatest in South Asia, Asia Pacific, and Sub-Saharan Africa (not sure why).

Hearing Loss and Deafness

Hearing losses may be mild, moderate, severe, or profound. It can affect one ear or both ears and can lead to difficulty in hearing conversational and understanding speech.

People with more significant hearing losses may benefit from cochlear implants. Deaf people mostly have profound hearing loss, which implies very little or no hearing. They often use sign language for communication. The causes of hearing loss and deafness can be congenital or acquired.

Congenital Causes of Hearing Loss

Congenital causes may lead to hearing loss being present at or acquired soon after birth. Hearing loss can be caused by hereditary and nonhereditary genetic factors or by certain complications during pregnancy and childbirth, including

- maternal rubella, syphilis, or certain other infections during pregnancy;
- low birth weight;

- birth asphyxia (a lack of oxygen at the time of birth);
- inappropriate use of particular drugs during pregnancy, such as aminoglycosides, cytotoxic drugs, antimalarial drugs, and diuretics;
- and severe jaundice in the neonatal period, which can damage the hearing nerve in a newborn infant.

Acquired Causes of Hearing Loss

Acquired causes may lead to hearing loss at any age, such as
- infectious diseases, including meningitis, measles, and mumps;
- chronic ear infections;
- collection of fluid in the ear (otitis media);
- use of certain medicines, such as those used in the treatment of neonatal infections, malaria, drug-resistant tuberculosis, and cancers;
- injury to the head or ear;
- excessive noise, including occupational noise, such as that from machinery and explosions;
- recreational exposure to loud sounds, such as that from use of personal audio devices at high volumes and for prolonged periods of time and regular attendance at concerts, nightclubs, bars, and sporting events;
- aging, in particular due to degeneration of sensory cells; and
- wax or foreign bodies blocking the ear canal.
- Among children, chronic otitis media is a common cause of hearing loss.

Functional Impact of Hearing Loss

One of the main impacts of hearing loss is on the individual's ability to communicate with others. Spoken language development is often delayed in children with unaddressed hearing loss. Unaddressed hearing loss and ear diseases, such as otitis media, can have a significantly adverse effect on the academic performance of children. They often have increased rates of grade failure and greater need for education assistance. Access to suitable accommodations is important for optimal learning experiences but are not always available.

Social and Emotional Impact of Hearing Loss

Exclusion from communication can have a significant impact on everyday life, causing feelings of loneliness, isolation, and frustration.

Economic Impact

WHO estimates that unaddressed hearing loss poses an annual global cost of US$750 billion. This includes health sector costs (excluding the cost of hearing devices).

In developing countries, children with hearing loss and deafness rarely receive any schooling. Adults with hearing loss also have a much higher unemployment rate.

Hearing loss represents the third most common problem with health in the United States, and it can affect the quality of one's life significantly. Around forty-eight million Americans have currently lost some of their hearing. One of the most common causes of hearing loss is advanced age. Around one in every three people between the ages of sixty-five and seventy-four will have some manner of hearing loss. Hearing loss is typically classified as mild, moderate, severe, and profound.

At one point, I envisioned I had a malignant tumor in my middle ear and looked to the the web for information. I learned that any malignant neoplasm involving the middle ear was nothing more than, according to the literature, "a pathologic curiosity."

So I continued my search, and I discovered knowledge that was again above my wildest dreams of ever finding. Particularly about the outer, middle, and inner sections of the ears.

Truths Discovered

It is my sincere hope that the facts discovered will help the world to understand the social, psychological, and well-being impacts on individuals, families, and communities who are faced with mild, moderate, or severe hearing losses.

To people who love to learn, you will gain a wealth of knowledge and facts about depression and cases of suicides told by relatives of people with hearing loss; nurses with hearing loss; loss of hearing in ancient times; myths to restore hearing loss; case studies; classroom strategies for hearing-loss teachers; difficulties hearing-loss people encounter while seeking health, help paying for hearing devices, and education; treatment of African American slaves; Gallaudet University before the Civil Rights Act of 1965; prisoners in penal systems with hearing loss or deafness; mental health care for the hearing-deficit person; making of the Americans with Disabilities Law; audiology departments housed in large medical centers; cochlear implants; hearing aids (invisible versus visible); ADA and caption calls; understanding denial, musical ears, or musical hallucinations; research being conducted to restore hearing loss; drugs to restore hearing; stem cells; microchips; regeneration of middle ear hair loss; robotic cars for the hearing-impaired; help paying for hearing aids; volunteer opportunities in hearing loss and deaf communities; sterilization and murder of disabled people during the Third Reich in Germany; and other truths about the treatment of the deaf and hard of hearing people.

CHAPTER 2

I had recently attended and delivered a presentation at a conference, before my hearing loss, entitled "Reasoning through the Logic of Global Health Care" at the International Conference on Critical Thinking and Educational Reform held in Berkeley, California. Entitled "Global Health Care Awareness." My presentation at the conference revolved around a previous lecture I had taught to senior-level nursing students enrolled in a community health nursing course.

The *framework* states that one can analyze the logic of anything through the use of elements of reasoning when it is applied to any concept, problem, textbook, article, situation, and/or particular course discipline.

There are eight elements (nonsequential) used to reason through the logic of anything by asking the following questions:

1. **Purpose—what is the purpose of my thinking or the author's purpose?**

   (e.g., comparison and contrast of health care in lesser developed countries and major health care organizations responsible for the implementation of global heath)

2. **Concepts—what are the concepts we're dealing with?**

   (*World Bank*—an agency related to the United Nations whose aim is lending money to lesser developing countries also involved in health projects to eradicate and control diseases

   Developed countries—countries with stable economic systems and technological development

   Less-developed countries—countries not yet stable economically or technologically)

   Nongovernmental organizations—help to provide 20 percent of all external aid to lesser developed countries, which are represented by many different religious and secular groups)

3. **Assumptions—what are the assumptions related to the problem?**

   (e.g., our world goes beyond the United States; a lot of diseases and disorders in third world countries will never be eradicated, so why bother)?

4. **Points of view—are there varying points of view regarding the problem?**

   (e.g., we are living in a global dynamic world with noticeable health disparities; it is therefore significant to think of health care in a global perspective rather than on a state or national level)

5. **Question—what are the questions surfacing regarding the issues?**

   (e.g., is it the responsibility of nurses to be concerned with the entire world's population and their healthcare? If so, why)?

6. **Information needed—what other information is needed to render logic to the problem?**

   (e.g., what role does the nursing profession has in promoting health and social justice within the framework of global health care?)

7. **Conclusion—what conclusions are reached?**

    (e.g., nurses will come in contact with clients from all over the world and therefore must be competent and skilled to educate all clients effectively)

8. **Implication—what are the evidence-based inferences?**

    (e.g., when evidence-based principles and concepts of global health care are practiced and applied by all health professionals throughout the world, positive outcomes are apt to occur locally, nationally, and worldwide)

    The presumption or idea of critical thinking according to scholars is that "Critical thinking cultivates the skills necessary for making responsible decisions that change the lives of individuals and transforms the world. While the liberal arts expose students to different ways of understanding the world and acting in it."

The Journey Begins

Upon my return to the university, while teaching a class to junior-level students on the subject of *critical thinking*, my loss of hearing came on suddenly, like a thief in the night, as I concluded the lecture and proudly proceeded to ask the class to raise their hands if they had questions.

One student with purple hair and dressed all in purple raised her hand. I smiled, making eye contact. As she proceeded to ask her question, I suddenly realized that I could see her lips moving but I literally I could not hear a word she was saying. I stared at her and asked that her question be repeated. She complied, and again, I could not hear a word she was saying. Her voice sounded totally garbled. I thought to myself, *Oh my god, I cannot hear! What is wrong with me? How on earth do I handle this situation?* I stood there in silence, trying to be in control.

All I could think to do at that moment was to inform the class that because of a previously ruptured eardrum (a lie), I was having some difficulty hearing their questions. I then instructed the class to write their questions on a piece of paper and to pass their written questions to the front of the class and that I would post each question with the answers on the blackboard for them to review.

I promptly dismissed the class. "See you next Thursday, and please use the remainder of class time for independent study." As I waited for the students to empty the classroom, I stood there mystified and musing as to why I suddenly lost my hearing and calling on the Almighty to *help* me.

Knowledge Is Truly Power

If I knew then what I know now, I would have made an appointment to see my internist immediately to discuss my hearing problem and to ask for an ENT referral to request that perhaps a steroid infusion be performed to possibly restore my hearing. Yet I did not think at the time to first see my internist to discuss the following options:

Steroid Infusions

A transtympanic steroid infusion is one of the possible options for patients with sudden sensorineural hearing loss in which local steroids are delivered into the ear in an attempt to reduce any inflammation that may have occurred there. The medication is infused into the middle ear. The aim is to recover some of the hearing loss that has occurred. People who experience a sudden hearing loss (SSNHL) are often treated with systemic steroids, which are typically taken orally. Studies, however, show that people with sudden sensorineural hearing loss (SSNHL) who do not respond to this treatment may benefit from intratympanic steroid injections.

Studies carried out at universities in the USA and Thailand show intratympanic steroid injections to be very effective and that the treatment does not have any side effects. The earlier the treatment, the better. As with systemic steroid treatment, the chances of recovery from sudden sensorineural hearing loss (SSNHL) are increased the earlier the treatment begins.

Denial

In the early stage of my hearing loss, I was in total *denial*. I flatly refused to succumb to my loss of hearing, but rather, I chose to continue to suffer in hearing loss silence. In some cases, initial short-term denial can be a good thing, giving you time to adjust to a painful or stressful issue in your life. It might also be a precursor to making some sort of change in your life. But denial also has a dark side.

Understanding Denial and Its Purpose

Refusing to acknowledge that something is wrong is a way of coping with emotional conflict, stress, painful thought, threatening information, and anxiety. Refusing to face facts may seem unhealthy. Sometimes, though, a short period of denial can be helpful. Being in denial gives your mind the opportunity to unconsciously absorb shocking or distressing information at a pace that won't send you into a psychological tailspin. For example, after a traumatic event, you might need several days or weeks to process what's happened and come to grips with the challenges.

As I continued my journey in denial, I forged ahead teaching as though everything was normal. One strategy I used during this period was to walk or sit closely among the students as I lectured to hear if students suddenly asked questions. It was a warm and fuzzy approach while it lasted.

Precipitously, after several months of faking it, I was lecturing in a large auditorium, standing in front of the class, feeling happy and secure as a normal person, forgetting that I had loss my hearing. At the very back of the auditorium, a student stood up (I nodded), and he began to ask a specific question regarding the lecture, Suddenly I remembered that I was not a normal hearing person but a hearing-loss person. The sound of his voice was garbled as I strained to really hear him. I quickly turned to the teaching assistant I had appointed earlier, cueing her to interpret for me, while again reminding the class of my "middle ear infection" and my "ruptured eardrum" (again a lie).

I asked the students to write their questions down on a piece of paper at the end of the lecture and said that my teaching assistant would collect their written questions as previously done in an earlier class. It was a perfect strategy … or so I thought.

As the course progressed, I continued to have students write their questions after each lecture, and I would post each student's question and the answer on the blackboard. It seemed like an ideal teaching strategy, or so I thought.

Faculty Evaluations

At the end of each course, students are asked to evaluate the professor's class. The process consists of sealed packets with a series of questions enclosed about the teacher's performance and the student learning outcomes. Teachers are asked to vacate the room during the evaluations; two students then collect the evaluations from students, place them in a sealed envelope, and take them to the head of the department's office. They are then forwarded to the *university researcher's* office to be tabulated, and the tallies are eventually returned to the faculty in a sealed envelope. Faculty evaluations are intended by the university as a tool for faculty to improve their teaching based on what the students are recommending or not recommending.

Shattered and Devastated

When I received my students' course evaluations from the institutional researcher; I sat quietly at my desk and began reading the students' comments. I suddenly felt a jolt, shattered and devastated to say the least. Their comments were brutal and merciless. While there were several negative comments, *the* most frequent devastating comment read as follows:

> Dear Professor,
>
> Why was this teaching strategy necessary: "having students write stupid questions on a stupid little piece of paper and passing them to you for posting?"
>
> This is really ridiculous, please try another approach—this is stupid.

Faculty Meetings

Another coping mechanism I employed was to sit next to the chairperson during weekly faulty meetings so I could hear the directives and tasks she delegated to the faculty and staff. Yet although we sat in a roundtable format, I still could not hear or understand every comment being discussed by the chairperson or other faculty members who sat directly in front or across the table from me.

Dean and the President's Meetings

These meetings were typically held in large auditorium settings; again, I could not hear what was being discussed throughout these meetings. I sat there for hours suffering in silence. I would rely on written minutes to find out what had been discussed and finalized.

Student Phone Calls

Student phone calls before and after classes during my office hours were painful. Students would call to discuss an assignment and/or a problem or concern. I devised a strategy where I would say to the students that there were problems with my phone and ask them to send me an email and that I would email my response.

CHAPTER 3

At the end of the academic year, I was totally exhausted. I suddenly realized that I had been in denial for some time about my hearing loss. I made the decision to seek professional medical help.

Acceptance

Self-acceptance comes from meeting life's challenges vigorously. Don't numb yourself to your trials and difficulties, nor build mental walls to exclude pain from your life. You will find peace not by trying to escape your problems, but by confronting them courageously. You will find fulfillment not in denial, but in the victory.

—J. Donald Walter

Medical Centers

It was during my summer vacation that I realized that I desperately needed some professional help; particularly after repeatedly having to ask family members and others to repeat what they were saying to me during conservations, and their responses were typically "Never mind." It was then that I decided to see a specialist about my hearing loss—namely, an otolaryngologist, a physician who provides comprehensive evaluation and services for patients with hearing loss. The department I selected was located in a large medical center in the inner city of Chicago: the *Northwestern Medical Center.*

History of Medical Centers

The world's first medical center to combine complete patient care, medical education, and research facilities in a single complex opened in 1928 (Columbia-Presbyterian Medical Center in New York). However, the *Texas Medical Center* located in Houston, Texas, is the largest of its kind in America. Not only does TMC have one of the highest volumes of clinical facilities for patient care, basic science, and research but it also houses two medical schools, four nursing schools, and one of the highest volumes of clinical facilities.

The Audiologist

My initial appointment was with an audiologist, an expert in the nonmedical testing and diagnosis of individuals experiencing hearing loss. She was a very pleasant and warm person, ideally suited for her role as a health professional. She introduced herself and proceeded to explain the procedure used to determine my hearing frequencies.

I was seated in a small booth with large earphones anchored to both of my ears as she sat in an adjacent glass-enclosed booth across from me and proceeded to test my hearing. I was then instructed to press a handheld button when I could hear the beeping sound. Portions of the beeps I could hear, and other beeping sounds I could barely hear. The test lasted approximately forty-five minutes. The audiologist presented a graphic printout of the results and explained the outcome of the test.

The Outcome

My hearing loss was determined to be such that I was a likely candidate for an implant. She stated that she would give the results to the physician and that he would discuss the surgical procedures involved in performing a cochlear implant. She asked if I had any questions: Once I regained my composure, I asked her to tell me more about *hearing aids*. She replied, "First of all, you need to know the following facts about hearing aids:

1. Hearing aids cannot restore your hearing or communications to normal as you remember.
2. Your voice will sound loud and unnatural. Hearing-impaired people tend to talk loudly in order to hear themselves.
3. A hearing aid is most effective when worn in quiet surroundings. No hearing aid eliminates background noise.
4. The further you are from the source, the less the hearing aids will work."

She ended the session by asking if I had further questions. I was thoroughly devastated, to say the least, and felt broken down, destroyed, and useless. I asked my inner voice, *How could I possibly continue teaching students how to care for patients?* I was totally devastated. I was given an appointment by the receptionist to see the otolaryngologist the following week. I quickly ran out of the medical center and into a waiting taxi.

The Otolaryngologist and Cochlear Implants

At home, I immediately turned on my computer to review again what this doctor's role was ("oto-what-cha-ma-call it"). The web search indicated that the otolaryngologist was a "surgical subspecialty within medicine that deals with conditions of the ear, nose, and throat and related structures of the head and neck.

Cochlear Implants

I became frightened and felt so lonely as I read that *cochlear implants* consisted of a medical device that bypasses damaged structures in the inner ear and directly stimulates the auditory nerve to improve hearing in people with severe or profound hearing losses. This creates a range of sound, but they do not replace normal hearing. I repeated over and over in my mind, *It does nothing to replace normal hearing. It does not replace normal hearing.* I dreaded the sheer thought of an upcoming appointment with the *cochlear implant surgeon.*

Enter the Dragon to Slay Me

The cochlear implant surgeon was a mild-mannered, friendly, and yet very serious individual. He introduced himself and asserted, "I hear you are a candidate for a cochlear implant? Well, you've come to the right place." Needless to say the least, I was not impressed but crushed. He proceeded to explain the procedure to me, never mentioning options other than a cochlear implant. In a stern and authoritarian stance without a pause, he proceeded to explain the cochlear procedure. I got the impression that cochlear implant surgeries were his whole purpose in life.

The Cochlear Implant Surgery

The surgery is usually performed as an outpatient procedure done under general anesthesia. "An incision is made behind the ear to open the mastoid bone leading to the middle ear space (an incision in the crease behind your ear). Once the middle ear space is exposed, an opening is made in the cochlea and the implant electrodes are inserted. This then requires a disk-shaped transmitter about an inch in diameter to be affixed to the outer surface of the skull, with a thin wire channeling down into a microphone looped around the patient's ear."

(To visualize the actual surgical procedures for cochlear implants, go to the web and click on "U-Tube - cochlear implant surgeries." (The procedure seen is graphic and bloody and may be disturbing to some—caution is *advised*).

Postoperatively

The surgeon went on to explain that most patients go home the same day and that the cutting behind the earlobe minimizes the visibility of the scar. To avoid disturbing the eardrum, an opening into the mastoid bone is made through which a bundle of electrodes are implanted into the cochlear, and the incision is closed with absorbable stitches that do not need to be removed. A dressing is then placed over the ear, and the patient is able to leave within three or four hours after surgery and can manage any pain with over-the-counter pain medication. *Oh really!* Your first follow-up visit is typically one week after surgery. The purpose of this visit is to check the incision.

My mood quickly turned to utter sadness and despair. I informed the surgeon at the conclusion of our conference that I needed time to think through this option. I quickly thanked him and literally ran out of the room and into a waiting elevator and out the door into a waiting yellow taxi.

As my hearing loss progressed and my ability to understand and communicate with others worsened, so did my depression. I found myself sleeping during the day and being awake during the night. I had loss of energy and even had thoughts of suicide and visualizing myself in a casket. Particularly, as I was visualizing the surgeon drilling in my inner ear and the thoughts of unbearable pain and suffering; I decided against the cochlear implant and would stick with hearing aids.

CHAPTER 4

Oralism versus Sign Language

Oralism is the education of deaf students through oral language by using lipreading, speech, and mimicking the mouth shapes and breathing patterns of speech.

Alexander Graham Bell—who gained fame, power, and wealth from his successful invention of the telephone—began promoting *oral education* as the superior educational option for deaf children. He traveled around the country giving speeches on the benefits of *oralism*. He was usually accompanied by deaf students who had learned to use speech.

Bell appealed to hearing parents who longed for their deaf children to speak and be like them. He argued that without speech, deaf children would never be able to participate fully in society. Politicians, educators, doctors, and wealthy hearing individuals took notice, and the campaign against American Sign Language and for the pure form of oralist method in deaf schools took off.

Alexander Graham Bell went on to argue against the use of *American Sign Language*. In regional residential schools, the development of deaf social clubs and programs and the exposure of young deaf children to deaf adults and administrators encouraged the pattern of deaf-deaf marriages to prevent the procreation of deaf children. He believed that by eliminating these factors and instead by using only local *oral education* in schools, deaf individuals would assimilate into mainstream hearing society and have more deaf-hearing marriages; this would decrease the number of deaf children born.

Congress of Milan

At the *Congress of Milan* at the end of the nineteenth century, educators of the deaf gathered from all over the world to discuss the future of deaf education. Due to his influence and wealth, Alexander Graham Bell presented for three days at this conference on the benefits of oral education for the deaf and the detriments of signed language. By contrast, advocates of sign language were only given three hours to make counterarguments.

At the end of the conference, all the attendees, none of them deaf, voted to ban teaching in sign languages in schools and prohibit its use in dormitories and endorsed oralism as the best educational method for the teaching of the deaf. This was the beginning of a one-hundred-year period in deaf history where children weren't allowed to use sign language in school or in the dorms.

American Sign Language was passed on secretly behind closed doors. Since then, the debate between *oralism* and *sign language* continues in medicine, education, and politics. Bell continues to influence the debate through the Alexander Graham Bell Association for the Deaf and Hard of Hearing whose mission is to advance listening and talking and early intervention for deaf and hard of hearing children and adults.

Mental Health Care for the Hearing-Impaired

Individuals who are deaf or hard of hearing experience the same mental health concerns as their hearing peers and, as such, seek out the same services to address these concerns. However, unlike hearing individuals, those who are deaf or hard of hearing do not always find equitable access to mental health services.

Services

Obtaining mental health services, while a personal and private decision, can also be very challenging—and especially challenging for people who are deaf or hard of hearing. An internet search reveals that mental health issues are perhaps more common among hard of hearing and deaf populations than those who can hear.

Although many deaf individuals lead healthy lives, some deaf individuals experience mental health concerns. Common referrals are for psychotherapy, also known as talk therapy or individual counseling, which includes clinical depression or overwhelming sadness, grief, and loss; anxiety, panic attacks, stress management; and sexual identity issues and/or deaf identity issues. Some deaf individuals do experience more serious mental disorders, including schizophrenia and bipolar disorder. Deaf individuals may also seek relationship or family conflicts or family trauma related to domestic violence.

Communicating with Deaf or Hard of Hearing Individuals

Communication barriers are the number 1 reason deaf people have poorer health compared to hearing people. Imagine not being able to understand what a doctor is telling you, how your medicines work, or why exactly you are taking pills. For that reason, it's vital that your surgery/hospital (not the patient) books an interpreter in advance of the patient's appointment. This is a basic right for deaf people and one that will ensure your patient has a clear understanding of their health and the information you are telling them.

Helpful Hints for Health Care Providers Include the Following:

1. Book an interpreter. Do not expect your patient to bring a friend or family member to interpret for them. They will not know medical jargon or be trained to interpret health information, but most importantly, your patient will have no independence or privacy if a friend or family member accompanies them.
2. If a patient brings a friend or family member into the appointment/doctor's room with them out of choice, do not talk to the friend or family person. Talk directly to your patient.
3. Make sure you have your patient's full attention before talking.
4. Maintain eye contact while communicating. Don't talk to your patient while looking at your computer screen, filling out paperwork, or turning around. Avoid covering your mouth with your hands or paper.

5. Use normal lip movement; you don't need to overexaggerate each word, and don't mumble. This makes it hard to lip-read.

6. Speak at a normal volume. Shouting can be uncomfortable for a patient wearing hearing aids. Make sure the room is well lit so that the patient can see your face clearly.

7. Speak in plain English at a normal speed.

8. If you are having difficulty explaining something, use written notes or diagrams to assist you.

9. Remember that all deaf people have different communication needs, so writing information down won't be helpful for everyone. If your patient doesn't understand you, try and think of a different way to explain yourself rather than repeating the same words again.

10. Use gestures and facial expressions to help explain yourself. Show with your face if something is painful, scary, or nothing to worry about.

11. Point to parts of your body if necessary.

12. Keep checking to make sure your patient understands you. If your patient doesn't understand you, try and think of a different way to explain yourself.

CHAPTER 5

One Thousand Years Before Christ

In historical stories of deafness and hard of hearing around 1000 BC, it has been recorded that a Hebrew law provided those with deafness and hearing loss limited rights to own property and marry. Deaf or hard of hearing people were considered to be subnormal by great philosophers such as Plato and Aristotle who are said to claim that those born with hearing disorders could not be educated and would become stupid and incapable of reasoning and that without the ability to hear, people could not learn.

Legends of Hard of Hearing and Deaf People

Brutal and violent stories have been recorded and is steeped in human existence. Evidence exists dating back to thirty-five to forty-five thousand years ago of hearing loss in Neanderthal skeletons. Some of our earliest evidence about hearing loss comes from the skeletal remains of ancient people who lived at least ten thousand years ago in what we now call Iraq and Kurdistan. There, remains of our human ancestors were found in Mount Bardot, an archaeological site. Some of these humans had bony growths in their ear canals—a condition called auditory exostoses, which, in severe forms, can impact people's abilities to hear. References to hearing loss were also made in Ancient Egypt, where a remedy for ears that hear badly calls for injecting olive oil, ant eggs, goat urine, bat wings, and red lead into a person's ear.

Hearing Loss in the Ancient Western World

People who were deaf and hard of hearing were long considered unintelligent or too simpleminded to be considered adults. These beliefs in the Western world date back to the teachings of Greek philosophers such as Plato and Aristotle in the tenth century. Their suggestions that reason and rationality were only available to those who could speak shaped much of the Enlightenment.

Hearing Loss and the American Civil War

The Civil War (1861–1865) in the United States represents the first time in history that a war provided an opportunity for deaf people to contribute meaningfully to a nation's welfare. Rather than on an organized level, hundreds of individual deaf men and women participated as soldiers, as journalists, and in a variety of other occupations either to preserve the Union or to secede from it.

Army regulations prevented men who were deaf from joining the army, but definitions of deafness were usually left up to the individual doctor carrying out medical exams. Hundreds of soldiers who were deaf managed to make it through medical examination and join both the Union and Confederate armies. The most famous of these were the Union's general John Gross Bernard, who was responsible for the construction of forts around Washington, DC, and on the Confederate side, General Maxcy Gregg, whose deafness is said to have caused his death at the Battle of Fredericksburg.

In a book written by Susan Rutherford entitled *A Study of American Deaf Folklore*. Accordingly, there was a time during the Civil War that both armies were running short of men. Both the Union and Confederate armies began recruiting *any able-bodied man* they could find—whether he could hear or not. So it happened that there were a Northern deaf soldier and Southern deaf soldier facing each other across the battlefield. The story goes that this one Northern soldier was very lonely. He could not sit and chat or interact with the other men in his company. Without any other deaf people there, he felt very isolated. At the same time, there was a Southern deaf soldier suffering the same feeling of loneliness and isolation. As was the case during the Civil War, the battle lines between the armies were often very close together. It was not uncommon for soldiers from both armies to talk to one another during a lull in the fighting.

One evening, the Northern deaf soldier decided to take a walk in the woods. To his shock, he came upon a Confederate soldier also on a walk through the woods. Both soldiers drew their guns on each other. One of the soldiers began to gesture nervously. The other recognized the signs and asked in sign language, "Are you deaf?"

The other soldier replied, "Yes! Yes!"

The first soldier signed, "Same as me. We are both deaf!"

"Same as me!" signed the second soldier.

Delighted to have found each other, they quickly put away their guns and began to talk and talk and talk.

Soon, some of the men from the Northern soldier's company noticed he was missing and sent out a party to look for him, as did the group from the Southern soldier's company. Both search parties happened upon the two deaf soldiers talking in the woods. Each group suspected espionage within their ranks, but no one knew who might be the spy. As both groups approached, the deaf soldiers quickly communicated, "No, no, we are deaf, that's all." They pleaded with their respective search parties to keep it a secret and not report them to their superiors. They were just happy to see another deaf person whom they could communicate with. They begged that their actions not be misunderstood and insisted they were not guilty of treason, a crime for which they would certainly be hanged. They so convinced the members of the search party that both groups stayed with the deaf men and socialized, ate, and drank together into the night. Afterward, each group went back to their respective camps.

The Plight of African American Slaves Hard of Hearing, Deaf, or Blind (1800–1865)

It can be said that the history of emancipation and reconstruction are based solely on an accounting of freed able-bodied slaves. Slaves with disabilities could not escape the plantation South if he or she were able to work.

"Sore Eyes"

It has been recorded in American slavery literature that among Southern slaves, of particular concern to slaveholders was blindness or sore eyes, which historians attributed to a vitamin A deficiency and was a widespread complaint on plantations in the South. It was a condition that was treated by physicians at the time with warm water and milk poultices. While not all blindness were caused by environmental factors or deficiencies, there were cases of congenital blindness as well.

The loss of vision, whether congenital or acquired, categorized a slave as falling within the realm of being "unsound" or unfit for labor. Plantation records, estate inventories, and insurance policies in the South indicates slaveholders typically assessed slaves with disabilities to be useless. For example, Honey, a fourteen-year-old girl who was hearing poor might have been listed for $150 lower than a sixteen-year-old because a slave who had trouble hearing would be more "difficult to discipline."

Following the Emancipation Proclamation, disabled slaves were virtually left enslaved under the control of plantation owners. This proves the extent to which the notion of freedom was consistently tied to questions of labor for all able-bodied slaves. It has been documented in slave literatures that helpless freed slaves were left on slave plantations and "still found support in their old homes." The fact that federal agents throughout the postwar South in county after county, state after state, encountered helpless slaves and did not liberate them from the plantations illustrates the extent to which *labor* was inextricably tied to ideas of freedom.

The Story of Blind Tom

When Tom was born on a Georgia plantation, his owner deemed him useless and not worth the effort—or expense—of feeding once he realized that the baby boy was blind. Tom, his mother, and two other children were soon sold to a Columbus lawyer named General James Bethune. Once he was exposed to the piano and the musical leanings of the Bethune children, Tom began to show an amazingly innate musical talent. He could mimic all sorts of sounds, both musical and nonmusical, and he could play back entire pieces of music after hearing them once.

The family that had bought Tom suddenly saw him as a gold mine rather than a useless mouth to feed, and they began sending him on tours throughout both the North and the South well into the Civil War. Proceeds from his performances went to the Confederate Army, and much of the money was used to care for the injured.

Unfortunately, Blind Tom also suffered from another undiagnosed disorder (in retrospect, many people believe he was autistic). His lack of maturity and emotional growth meant that even after the Civil War, he still needed a guardian to manage his performances, tours, and finances; when he died in 1908, he still lived in the Hoboken home of Eliza Bethune. Sometimes called the last slave, Blind Tom's ability to touch people through his music was undeniable. He played for President James Buchanan at the White House at a time when it was unheard of for any slave to use anything but the back door. Mark Twain wrote of his abilities, going to performance after performance. And when he was fifteen, Tom composed what would be his most famous piece: "Battle of Manassas."

Thus, the slavery system was based on the master slaveholders' premise that if a slave was able-bodied—be he or she deaf, hard of hearing, blind, or crippled but fit and able to contribute economically to the overall plantation—then he or she was considered worthy of feeding, clothing, and controlling.

Discrimination against Deaf and Hard of Hearing African Americans

Discriminatory practices can be traced back to the segregation era during the seventeenth to mid-twentieth centuries. Black deaf individuals were not accepted in either the *deaf* or the *African American* community. Black deaf students were prohibited from opportunities to interact with students and teachers on the white deaf school campuses; this separation contributed to the development of Black African American sign language, a dialect of American Sign Language that's distinctly different.

Gallaudet University

Gallaudet University is a federally chartered private university for the education of the deaf and hard of hearing located in Washington, DC. Founded in 1864, Gallaudet University was originally for both deaf and blind children. Gallaudet University is the premier institution of learning, teaching, and research for deaf and hard of hearing students throughout the world.

Gallaudet was the first school for the advanced education of the deaf and hard of hearing in the world and remains the only higher education institution in which all programs and services are specifically designed to accommodate deaf and hard of hearing students. Hearing students are admitted to the graduate school, and a small number are also admitted as undergraduates each year. The university was named after Thomas Hopkins Gallaudet, a notable figure in the advancement of deaf education who himself was *not* deaf. Before the Civil Rights Act of 1965, Gallaudet University—then a college—did not admit Black students.

Hearing Loss in Modern History

Everyone knows about Alexander Graham Bell and his invention of the telephone. Many people do not know that he was also a deaf educator, and his methods (and reasons behind those methods) continue to cause controversy in the deaf community today.

Alexander Graham Bell was a staunch believer in *eugenics*. In 1883, Alexander Graham Bell delivered an address to the National Academy of Sciences entitled "Memoir upon the Formation of a Deaf Variety of the Human Race." In this presentation and publication, he discussed the high rates of deaf-deaf marriages and how it increases the number of deaf children through the passing on of generational deafness. Alexander Graham Bell argued that this phenomenon was creating a deaf race that shares a language and culture. He said, "Those who believe as I do, that the production of a defective race of human beings would be a great calamity to the world." Bell strongly opposed intermarriage among congenitally deaf people. He feared "contamination" of the human race by the propagation of deaf people even though most deaf people statistically are born to hearing parents.

Suggestions were made to enact legislation to prevent the <u>intermarriage of deaf-mute people</u> or to forbid marriage between families that have more than one deaf-mute member. In his paper, he proposed to reduce the number of the deaf by discouraging deaf-mute to deaf-mute marriages, advocating speech reading and articulation training for an oral-only method of education, removing deaf teachers and sign language.

Deaf and Hard of Hearing Humans in Nazi Germany (1933–1945)

If you were born deaf or hard of hearing and a female in Germany during the rise of the Third Reich, you would probably be sterilized as a eugenics measure to ensure control over women *not* to give birth to a deaf or hard of hearing baby. Historical accounts of the Holocaust reveal the atrocities of the Third Reich against human beings during Hitler's reign.

When the Nazis assumed power in Germany in 1933, they wasted no time in implementing their radical policies, first by securing passage of the law for the prevention of offspring with hereditary diseases. Among those designated by this law as congenitally disabled were deaf people who shared the fate of all persons with mental and physical disabilities, such as physical and cognitive disabilities, homosexuals, alcoholics, prostitutes, illegitimately born, criminals, those suffering from transmitted diseases or tuberculosis, the poor, and those considered lazy or shiftless.

In 1939, the Nazis' racial hygiene or euthanasia program murdered disable children *first*, using barbiturate overdose or starvation. The killing of adults followed the killing of infants and young children".

Sterilizations in Nazis Germany

Sterilizations of humans were done through surgical procedures, x-rays, or supercooled carbon dioxide injected into the fallopian tubes of women (scarring of the fallopian tubes). It has been estimated that 350,000 to 400,000 people were sterilized in Germany. Doctors, nurses, and other health care professionals were deeply involved in the killing of disabled people. Doctors trained in anthropology performed all "selection" at the death camps. Organs were taken for "scientific" studies. The brain was in greatest demand. The looting was by so-called scientists who traveled extensively to find victims who could be murdered for their brains.

To implement the killing of disabled people, according to documents of the terror, Hitler appointed senior officials to organize and direct the killings. The offices of the facilities were located in Berlin on Tiergartenstrasse 4, a killing enterprise known as *Operation T4*. Hitler labeled these killings "mercy deaths."

Deaf People in American Prisons (2018–2019)

The United States hold the largest prison population in the world, holding more humans than any other nation on earth. The majority of those confined, according to prison documents, are Black or Brown and poor. Data indicates that Black and Latinos make up 72 percent of federal and state prison populations.

Fast forward to the twenty-first century and zero in on the American penal systems. The present population of prisoners in American penal systems has soared. There are tens of thousands of deaf people in jails and prisons across America. Most correctional facilities do not track the numbers or locations of deaf prisoners.

While in jails and prisons, people are faced with personal disability and injustices daily. A person is hard of hearing if he or she has a 50 percent loss of hearing in one ear. Prisoners who are illiterate as well as deaf are especially deprived when they find themselves in the criminal justice system. They seldom have been educated beyond second grade and, as a consequence, have trouble reading and writing. Because they are deaf and without competent interpreters, they can't go to AA meetings or drug counseling or make it through educational programs. The abuses are said to begin as soon as a deaf prisoner faces accusers in court. Often the hard of hearing and deaf can't hear the charges against them, don't know what the trial is all about, don't know why the guards are screaming at them, and can't hear bells or commands from others. If they are close enough to the judge and look hard at him, they may be able to read his or her lips.

Prisons across the US routinely, while professing the Americans with Disabilities Act, are subjecting thousands of inmates with physical and mental health problems to painful and sometimes humiliating conditions.

Case Study

Alleged violations include a case in Washington State where an inmate with neuropathy, a nerve condition that can cause numbness in the hands and feet, ended up living on the floor of his cell in solitary confinement. The prisoner, fifty-year-old Curtis Graham, claimed he was forced to urinate in cups because he was unable to stand after prison staff changed his medication and confiscated his orthopedic shoes and cane.

Jails and prisons are required to provide necessary devices such as canes, walkers, catheters, bags, wheelchairs, hearing aids, medications, and orthopedic shoes. On the other hand, inmates who are deaf or hard of hearing typically endure the following:

- Lack of qualified interpreters available.
- Deaf prisoners are only allowed one hearing aid even if two are needed. Hearing-impaired prisoners are limited to two batteries per hearing aid per month.
- The use of sign language is prohibited in some prisons and oftentimes viewed as gang signs.
- Deaf and hard of hearing prisoners are oftentimes punished for not responding to verbal orders when, in fact, their batteries are dead and they simply cannot hear.

CHAPTER 6

Global Embrace of Deaf and Loss of Hearing Cultures

Globally, different deaf cultures have emerged and developed complex methods for communicating. These communities are often fostered in deaf schools that take deaf and hard of hearing people seriously.

In America and around the world, we are embracing the civil rights of deaf people, and the hard of hearing are being recognized through closed-captioned telephones, phones, closed-captioned television, *signing* interpreters for all special events and emergency held news reports.

Future Shock

I predict that by the year 2030 or sooner, there will be special restaurants, movie theaters, bars, medical clinics, and other public places specifically designed for deaf and hard of hearing people.

I also envision deaf and hard of hearing elected officials serving as senators and house of representative members in state and federal governments or even an *elected deaf president of the United States*.

CHAPTER 7

Tinnitus, Depression, and Suicides

At one point during my deep descent into hearing loss, I felt so alone and lonely and depressed that I sought respite through reading books. During the summer and fall of 1998–2000, I read a total of over twenty-seven books. I scoured bookstores like on a hunt for lost treasures. Perhaps some of the most memorable books, to name a few, included *Tell My Sons* by Mark Weber (2012); *Deaf People in Hitler's Europe* by Donna Ryan (2002); *Giving through Teaching by* Fitzpatrick, Shultz, and Aiken (2010); *African American Slavery and Disability* by Dea Boster (2013); *Mommy, What's That Number on Your Arm? A-6374* by Gloria Hollander Lyon (2016); and *The Death of.*

As I read, I can hear the voices of each writers, for I read to hear and hear as I read. As I searched for ways to escape my terrible suffering from loneliness and depression, I held all writers in deep esteem and I paid homage to each writer who took the time to write and enlighten the world.

"Books are the most acceptable ways of ignoring life". With each book I read, my inner reading voice allowed me to engage in a conversation with the authors. I was able to speak without any interruptions by hearing the other person saying "Never mind" to me if I didn't understand what the authors were writing about. Perhaps the greatest reward through reading is the wealth of knowledge gained about so many cultures, geographies, diseases, and human influence.

Depression and Suicide

Depression is the leading cause of disability among adults, affecting over fifteen million, and hearing loss is the second. Both depression and hearing loss have been linked with social, personal, and economic problems. Depression caused by any chronic disease often makes the condition worse, especially if the illness limits a person's ability to interact with others. Anytime a person suffers a bodily loss, such as a loss of hearing, depression is inevitable.

While the depression took hold of my psyche and thoughts of suicide danced inside my cerebrum, I vowed to stay strong and continued to prepare weekly lesson plans for the courses I was assigned to teach, which included

1. leadership and management,
2. introduction to health professions (two sections),
3. fundamentals of nursing (team-taught), and
4. a graduate-level course entitled "Health Policy and Nursing."

As a student intern on the psychiatry ward, I recalled counseling suicide patients not to think of destroying themselves but to engage in therapeutic activities (a *misnomer*).

Suicide

Over 50 percent out of twenty-five thousand people who die by suicide suffer from major depression. If one includes alcoholics who are depressed, this figure rises to over 75 percent. Depression affects nearly 5–8 percent of Americans ages eighteen and over in a given year. Twenty-five million Americans suffer from depression each year. Over 50 percent of all people who die by suicide suffer from major depression.

Beethoven

One can only imagine the frustration and anguish one feels when faced with the loss of hearing as did Beethoven, who was only twenty-nine when he faced this severe crisis. His deafness was an attack on his very being, his very existence, greatly impeding his ability to create. Unable to hear the notes he played, he would rest his head on the piano so he could feel their vibration.

Between April and October 1802, Beethoven wrote a final letter to his brothers, Carl and Johann, in which he explained his "wretched existence" and his terrible sense of isolation and despair and contemplating suicide. He eventually decided against suicide, and he went on to compose the greatest musical master pieces in the world.

Tinnitus (Ringing in the Ear) and Suicide

Tinnitus sufferers hear a persistent noise in one or both ears that comes from inside the body. The irritating sound can be low- or high-pitched buzzing and ringing. Studies have found that deaf individuals have higher rates of psychiatric disorder than those who are hearing while at the same time encountering difficulties in accessing mental health services. The web is filled with stories of suicides because of individuals suffering from tinnitus, the constant ringing in the ears, and the ideations of suicides.

Eric Clapton, the world-famous musician and guitarist, has revealed that he is losing his hearing. The great seventy-two-year-old guitarist admitted that he's struggling with tinnitus, a ringing in the ear commonly caused by noise-induced hearing loss. Combined with ongoing nerve damage that has affected his back and movement in his hands, he admits that live concerts have become a challenge. Even so, he says he intends to continue performing. "I am still going to work. I'm doing a few gigs. I am going to do a show at Hyde Park [British Summer Time festival] in July," he says. "The only thing I'm concerned with now is being in my seventies and being able to be proficient. I mean, I'm going deaf, I've got tinnitus, my hands just about work. I mean, I am hoping that people will come along and see me [for] more than [because] I am a curiosity. I know that is part of it, because it's amazing to *myself* that I am still here."

CHAPTER 8

Nurses with Hearing Loss

According to the American Academy of College of Nursing (2011), there are more than three million licensed nurses in this country. If hearing loss statistics for nurses are similar to the 15–17 percent prevalence rates of the general population, there are approximately 450,000 to more than half a million registered nurses who are working with hearing loss.

Consider the case of a student enrolled in nursing school who was a hearing-disabled person because they say she was not able to care for patients.

Case Study

Jessica Wells had always wanted to be a nurse. In 2006, she applied to the Associate Science in Nursing (ASN) program at Cox College in Springfield, Missouri. Unfortunately, her GPA wasn't high enough to make the cut, so she enrolled as a general education student, hoping to improve her grades. Wells, who is deaf, flourished, thanks in part to the accommodations that the college provided to her, such as volunteer notetakers and interpreters who accompanied her to class.

After college administrators asked an employee to shadow Wells to determine how a hearing-loss person would fare as a nursing student, the employee reported that "the deaf/hard-of-hearing individual can be successful as both a nursing student and a nurse." Wells, then in her midtwenties, was accepted into the ASN program in fall 2007. She had an American Sign Language (ASL) interpreter with her in class, in pre- and postclinical conferences, and for a week of rotations with real patients.

On January 22, however, just before the spring 2008 semester began, Wells received a letter from the school dismissing her from the program. The college asserted that her hearing loss would substantially limit (and, in some cases, completely limit) Well's ability to safely perform clinical rotations.

On January 21, 2009, Wells filed a petition in the Circuit Court of Greene County. She claimed that her dismissal from the program violated the Americans with Disabilities Act (ADA) because the school "fail [end] to provide plaintiff with reasonable accommodations so that she could participate in its nursing program despite her disability."

"She'd done just fine in her clinical training," says attorney Rita Sanders. "The school's decision had no grounds." The college replied, arguing that the need to have interpreters in the clinical setting posed a "direct threat to the health or safety of patients."

Case Interpretations

Did Cox College discriminate against a deaf student by dismissing her from its nursing program? (You be the judge.) Major barriers that prevent nursing students with disabilities from being accepted into nursing programs include the following:

1. Outmoded admission standards that deter applicants with disabilities
2. Fallacies about the capacity of students with disabilities to function effectively in the clinical components of nursing education
3. Lack of a comprehensive understanding of issues related to patient care

Despite the unique perspective and set of skills that students and health professionals with disabilities have to address many of these challenges, people with disabilities—in many instances—are often excluded from admission into nursing education programs and the nursing profession.

Researchers have found that nurses with disabilities often leave the nursing profession because they feel discriminated against or they fear they will jeopardize patient safety. However, there are no documented incidents of patient injury related specifically to a nurse's disability. To date, several exploratory research studies focusing on nurses with physical and/or sensory disabilities have demonstrated that these nurses experience discrimination in the workplace.

Nursing because they feel they are not supported by colleagues and administrators *or* they are unaware of their legal rights. The nurse recruiters commented that they weren't aware of having interviewed any nurses with disabilities and admitted that a nurse with a disability might not receive a reasonable accommodation despite the mandates of the Americans with Disabilities Act.

CHAPTER 9

The Making of the Americans with Disabilities Act

The Americans with Disabilities Act (ADA) prohibits discrimination against people with disabilities. The law made it illegal to discriminate against a disabled person in terms of employment opportunities, access to transportation, public accommodations, communications, and government activities. The law prohibits private employers, state and local governments, employment agencies, and labor unions from discriminating against the disabled. Employers are required to make reasonable accommodations in order for a disabled person to perform their job function.

Americans with Disabilities

The act (ADA) is a federal legislation passed in 1990. Conditions that rise to the level of a disability include the following: deafness or hard of hearing, blindness, intellectual disability, mental illness, partially or completely missing limbs, mobility impairments, autism, cancer, cerebral palsy, diabetes, epilepsy, addictions, hypertension, or digestive disorders. Thus, the Americans with Disabilities Act can be said to embrace the very foundation and definition of human rights.

What Are Human Rights?

Human rights are rights inherent to all human beings regardless of gender, nationality, place of residency, sex, ethnicity, religion, color, and other categorization. Thus, human rights are nondiscriminatory, meaning that all human beings are entitled to them and cannot be excluded from them. Of course, while all human beings are entitled to human rights, not all human beings experience them equally throughout the world. The process of making laws in Washington, DC, is often seen as complex and confusing, causing some people to shy away from the meaning and purposes for which legislations are enacted by the Congress and signed into law by the president of the United States.

Article I section 7 of the US Constitution states that "Every bill which shall have passed the House of Representatives and the Senate, shall, before it becomes a law, be presented to the President of the United States; if he approves he signs it, but if not he shall return it, with his/her objections …"

The ADA Story

The ADA story began a long time ago in cities and towns throughout the United States when people with disabilities began to challenge societal barriers that excluded them from their communities and when parents of children with disabilities began to fight against the exclusion and segregation of their children. It began with the establishment of local groups to advocate for the rights of people with disabilities. It began with the establishment of the independent-living movement that challenged the notion that people with disabilities needed to be institutionalized and that fought for and provided services for people with disabilities to live in the community.

The ADA owes its birthright not to any one person, or any few, but to the many thousands of people who make up the disability rights movement—people who have worked for years organizing and attending protests, licking envelopes, sending out alerts, drafting legislation, speaking, testifying, negotiating, lobbying, filing lawsuits, being arrested, and doing whatever they could for a cause they believed in. There are far too many people whose commitment and hard work contributed to the passage of this historic piece of disability civil rights legislation to be able to give appropriate credit by name. Without the work of so many—without the disability rights movement—there would be no ADA.

Injustices Overturned

The disability rights movement, over the last couple of decades, has made the injustices faced by people with disabilities visible to the American public and to politicians. This required reversing the centuries-long history of out of sight, out of mind that the segregation of disabled people served to promote. The disability rights movement adopted many of the strategies of the civil rights movements before it.

Like the African Americans who sat in at segregated lunch counters and refused to move to the back of the bus, people with disabilities sat in federal buildings, obstructed the movement of inaccessible buses, and marched through the streets to protest injustice. And like the civil rights movements before it, the disability rights movement sought justice in the courts and in the halls of Congress.

Section 504 of Rehabilitation Act

From a legal perspective, a profound and historic shift in disability public policy occurred in 1973 with the passage of Section 504 of the 1973 Rehabilitation Act. Section 504, which banned discrimination on the basis of disability by recipients of federal funds, was modeled after previous laws that banned race, ethnic origin, and sex-based discrimination by federal fund recipients. For the first time, the exclusion and segregation of people with disabilities was viewed as discrimination. Previously, it had been assumed that the problems faced by people with disabilities, such as unemployment and lack of education, were inevitable consequences of the physical or mental limitations imposed by the disability itself. After Section 504 established the fundamental civil right of nondiscrimination in 1973, the next step was to define what nondiscrimination meant in the context of disability. How was it the same or different from race and sex discrimination? The Department of Health, Education, and Welfare (HEW) had been given the task of promulgating regulations to implement Section 504.

People with disabilities sat in at HEW buildings. The longest sit-in was in San Francisco, lasting twenty-eight days. A lawsuit was filed, hearings before Congress were organized, testimony was delivered to congressional committees, negotiations were held, and letters were written. The disability community mobilized a successful campaign using a variety of strategies, and on May 4, 1977, the Section 504 regulations were issued. It is these regulations that form the basis of the ADA. In the early 1980s, the disability community was called upon to defend the hard-fought-for Section 504 regulations from attack.

Disability Coalitions

After a remarkable show of force and commitment by the disability community, the administration announced a halt to all attempts to deregulate Section 504. This was a tremendous victory for the disability movement. During much of the 1980s, the disability community's efforts in Washington were focused on reinstating civil rights protections.

Supreme Court Decisions

Southeastern Community College v. Davis US 397

During the 1980s, it also became clear to the disability community that it should play a very active role in Supreme Court litigation under Section 504. The first Section 504 case that was decided by the Supreme Court in 1979—*Southeastern Community College v. Davis, 442 US 397*—revealed, at best, a lack of understanding and, at worst, a hostility toward even applying the concept of discrimination to exclusion based on disability.

Case Study

A hearing-impaired woman was seeking admission to the nursing program of Southeastern Community College. The court found that Ms. Davis's hearing impairment rendered her unqualified to participate in the program because she would not be able to fully fulfill all the clinical requirements. However, the court did not limit itself to the fate of Ms. Davis but included within the decision several very broad negative interpretations of Section 504. In fact, the Davis decision cast doubt on whether those entities covered by Section 504 would be required to take any affirmative steps to accommodate the needs of persons with disabilities. Contrary to established court doctrine, the Section 504 regulations that had been issued by the Department of Health, Education, and Welfare (HEW) were given little deference by the court. Ironically, the court attributed this lack of deference to the fact that the HEW had been recalcitrant in issuing the regulations. After the Davis decision, it was clear that the Supreme Court needed to be educated on the issue of disability-based discrimination and the role that it plays in people lives.

Heartbreaking Testimonies

The witnesses spoke of their own experiences with discrimination. A young woman who had cerebral palsy told the senators about a local movie theater that would not let her attend because of her disability. When her mother called the theater to protest that this attitude sounded like discrimination, the theater owner stated, "I don't care what it sounds like." This story became a symbol for the ADA and was mentioned throughout the floor debates and at the signing. The members and the president related this story to demonstrate that America did care what it'd sound like and would no longer tolerate this type of discrimination.

A Vietnam veteran who had been paralyzed during the war and came home using a wheelchair testified that when he got home and couldn't get out of his housing project or on the bus or off the curb because of inaccessibility and couldn't get a job because of discrimination, he realized he had fought for everyone but himself—and he vowed to fight tirelessly for the passage of the Americans with Disabilities Act.

The president of Gallaudet College gave a compelling testimony about what life was like for someone who was deaf, faced with pervasive communication barriers. The audience was filled with Gallaudet students who waved their hands in approval. A woman testified that when she lost her breast to cancer, she also lost her job and could not find another one as a person with a history of cancer. Parents whose small child had died of AIDS testified they couldn't find any undertaker to bury their child.

While some in the media portrayed this new era as falling from the sky unannounced, the thousands of men and women in the disability rights movement knew that these rights were hard-fought for and were long overdue. The ADA is radical only in comparison to a shameful history of outright exclusion and segregation of people with disabilities. From a civil rights perspective, the Americans with Disabilities Act is a systematization of simple justice.

Chapter 10

Musical Ear Syndrome

Next to the Word of God, the noble art of music is the greatest treasure in the world.

—Martin Luther

The Ghost in Our Ears: The Sound of Music

Eric Clapton's "Change the World," Bob Marley's "I Shot the Sheriff," Artie Shaw's "Begin the Beguine," Z. Z. Hill singing "Down Home Blues," and Mahalia Jackson's "In the Upper Room" are all but faded memories of songs I love and could once hear with precision and clarity; and the sound of the lyrics are garbled, unclear voices by the musical artist. All distant memories that I would give anything to be able to hear clearly just one more time.

In the still of the night, as I lay awake and unable to sleep, I could hear the sound of repeated melodies being played over and over again in my ears or the sounds of an airplane engine or a diesel truck idling far away in the distance. Initially I thought my hearing was being restored, and so I embraced the sounds. But when the music and the engine sounds became a constant in my ears, I thought I was losing my mind and wished I could turn the sounds off.

I searched relentlessly to find any information to help me understand what was happening; I envisioned that my hearing was being restored, but I found zilch. Instead I discovered a website called the Musical Ear Syndrome. *Wow!* I thought to myself, *Oh, will I be able to hear music again?* But then my inner voice spoke loud and clear, *No, dear professor Juanita, you will never ever again hear the sound of music as you did when hearing was normal.* (Despair.)

The literature is filled with persons describing what is referred to as musical ear syndrome (MES), a condition referred to as auditory hallucinations of complex music, singing, and phantom voices (nonpsychiatric in nature). Social media sites are replete with testimonies of individuals who profess to experience musical ear syndrome, some of which I have recorded from internet testimonies:

Little says:

"I am 81 years old, I gradually lost my hearing. The worst part of it is, I am not able to listen to music. The sounds are of pitch. I had tinnitus for years and I kind of accepted that. Now I am having MES. Of course at first I thought I was losing my mind. I didn't want to tell anybody."

Sharon says:

"I hear Christmas Carols and some patriotic music. At times songs play I've never heard before, vocal and all. I am a writer, *Beautiful Dreamer* has been playing. I have written songs in the past. I don't know, but this might be a new beginning for me … Now if I can just figure out how to write the words down as they play …"

Keith says:

"I am 70 years old and have gone from normal hearing (60 years) to the point where I am virtually deaf. I've had a cochlear implant for a little over a year. About 4 months ago I suddenly developed Musical Ear Syndrome and have experienced music constantly since. I am able to switch from one tune to another at will. The music sounds orchestral. I go from children's songs to classical to hymns to pop. The music does seem to stop when I sleep but it resumes immediately when I awake. I have always been a music lover and the loss of the ability to enjoy music was extremely distressing. Before I (recently) learned about MES, I assumed that my brain was simply trying to fill the void left by my hearing loss."

T Dill says:

"I am currently 43 years old and diagnosed with vestibular vertigo by a hearing specialist. I often get dizzy and nauseous with migraine, and hear strange noises. My kids tell me I'm nuts. The noises range from repeatedly hearing an old fashioned 70s type telephone ringing, a small child calling out "mom" (my sons have manly voices now and are over 16) banging noises when I'm asleep, and whooshing sounds like noises in utero. Occasionally I hear music like pop tunes, but I can tune it out watching movies or TV shows, but still watch them closed captioned, because I miss what's being said in a quiet scene. I am glad I'm not alone in this, but it's very eerie and troublesome and there is no cure."

Theoretical Explanations of Musical Ear Syndrome

This phantom sound (MES) is akin to the same sensation patients who have had a leg amputated experience—the sensation that an amputated or missing limb is still attached.

Thus, the phantom hearing sound originates from the brain because of the "amputated or cut off of the loss of hearing from the middle ear to the brain," resulting in the phantom musical sounds being heard by people with hearing loss … *wow!*

Another theory is the release phenomenon MES is caused by hypersensitivity in the auditory cortex of the brain caused by sensory deprivation, secondary to their hearing loss. This "hole" in the hearing range is "plugged" by the brain confabulating a piece of information—in this case, a piece of music.

I sit and wonder why God chose to take away my hearing, and I pray:

> Oh, God, please grant me the serenity to accept the things I cannot change and the
> courage to change the things I can and, with wisdom, to know the difference.

CHAPTER 11

Scientist Race to Restore Hearing Loss

Hair Cells

We are each born with about fifteen thousand hair cells in each ear, but once these hair cells are damaged, these hair cells cannot regrow. However, researchers are testing how to regrow hair cells in the middle ear. Other scientists are experimenting with regrowing new hair on balding men and women, so why not grow new hairs in the inner ear to restore hearing?

Scientists have managed to create skin in a lab, complete with hair follicle. Scientists, for the first time, have grown both the upper and lower layers, known as the epidermis and dermis respectively, marking the first time a skin model has been made so closely resembling natural hair than any previous treatment. The new skin model could also prove useful. Stem cell therapy has been suggested as a possible future treatment for hair loss for years for both men and women. Is it not possible for scientists to experiment with growing hair cells in the inner ear?

These thousands and thousands of tiny nerves called *hair cells*, which line the inside of the snail-shaped structure of the cochlea, causes a person to lose their hearing when they are damaged. If scientists can help humans replace lost hair cells in the inner ear, we may one day be able to regain our lost hearing. The cochlear hair cells do not regenerate, so right now, damage to them is permanent and common among people with various types of hearing loss. But that may not always be the case. Researchers, in America and around the world, have developed a technique to stimulate progenitor hair cells in the inner ear—growing two thousand times more hair cells than previously possible. Scientists throughout the world are perfecting ways to develop new discoveries, opening paths to treatments for hearing loss.

Drugs

Using a *drug cocktail*, researchers can now grow in a petri dish colonies of sound-sensing hair cells with intricate hair bundles (cyan) from a single cochlear hair cell. This finding is said to accelerate research and lead to the development of new therapies for hearing loss.

Remarkable progress has been made, bringing us to a point where there are a number of promising new treatments for hearing loss and tinnitus being clinically tested. According to a host of scientists in California, "We're about to enter a new exciting era where people confronting hearing loss won't just be limited to hearing implants". Drug treatments are within touching distance.

Stem Cell

A new study led by scientists at Rutgers University–New Brunswick has demonstrated an exciting new gene therapy treatment that stimulates inner ear stem cells into becoming auditory neurons. The technique could potentially reverse hearing loss in many people, but the researchers urge caution, as the stimulation of these stem cells could also have major side effects, such as increased cancer risk. This study offers scientists working with stem cell therapies a fair warning into how the treatment can be a double-edged sword cell research; it is a strong reminder that there is still a great deal of work to do before it is deemed absolutely safe.

Microchips

Scientist are soon to develop microchips programmed to convert sensor sounds into word translations through implanted chips in the cochlear, just as cars without humans are being driven through robotic sensors. In 2016, seven states (Nevada, California, Florida, Hawaii, Michigan, Washington, and Tennessee) and the District of Columbia have enacted laws for "without steering wheels, foot pedals, mirrors, and human drivers, behind the wheel" are being tested.

Ear, nose, and throat researchers at major universities around the world have developed microphones that can be implanted in the middle ear to restore hearing that requires no clunky external electronics—a device that has improved hearing but requires a microphone and related electronics to be worn outside the head. Whereas, biomedical engineers and scientists are currently experimenting with tested implanted microchips in the ear canals of cadavers. It is mind-boggling to think that in the not so near future, all hearing-loss persons would only need a microchip implanted in their middle ear to hear the sounds of the world once again—without having to attach hearing devices to their outer ears. To think that a microchip placed in the inner ear would be all that's needed to hear voices/sounds. The microchip device would rely on eardrum vibrations in order to function. Once electrical signals are activated, the microchip would then route these signals to electrodes embedded in the cochlear. The cochlear nerves would then transmit messages to the brain to analyze and decipher sounds. In addition to the implant, there would be a charger device for the microchip. The charger does not need to be plugged into an outlet in order to do its job. Instead, it can draw its energy from a common cell phone. The implant would run on an implanted battery. This battery's power would be replenished overnight by a charger attached to the patient's ear. This charger would be able to supply the chip with eight hours of power in minutes. Researchers hope that the charger will provide the implant with several days of power—not unbelievable if we can sit and watch a Super Bowl football game played thousands of miles away and see the actions and movements of each of the players from start to finish of the games.

Dragon

The Dragon transcription solution is yet another invention for the hard of hearing professor who is hard of hearing and needs to record lectures, student grievances, faculty meetings, conference meetings, and other digital voice recordings to be transcribed into written documents. Yes, the Dragon will transcribe any single-recorded audio files to your PC or MAC into a written transcript (unbelievable).

Robotic Cars

Will driverless cars hold promise for people with hearing loss, cochlear implants, and hearing aids? Especially individuals who are born deaf? It is very hard to understand them when they speak. Would people who have been deaf since birth or who are dependent on lipreading have any way of telling the car what to do? Turning the wheels over to a robotic driver is a daunting challenge, and yet scientific developers are likely to develop a fool-proof *driverless car* in the near future.

CHAPTER 12

Balance, Dizziness, and Vertigo

When I think of balance, I think of my checkbook and the balance in my account. Since the loss of my hearing, the term "balance" has taken on a whole new meaning and is no longer centered on the balance in my checking account. *Webster* defines "balance" as a state of steadiness, stability, or equilibrium.

One of the most emotional painful time of my hearing loss journey relates to the dizziness and vertigo and the loss of balance I experienced constantly. I was fearful of falling facedown whenever I picked up an object off the floor.

It all started one morning as I ventured out into the streets of Chicago, walking down State Street toward Starbucks to get a cup of coffee and to just sit, relax, and people-watch. As I was walking on the sidewalk, I found myself gravitating literally, bumping into other people as if in a drunken haze and feeling dizzy. Having taught anatomy and physiology over the years, I instinctively knew that the function of the cerebellum portion of my brain, located in the back of my head, played a very vital part of motor control, muscle tone, equilibrium, and balance as it relates to movement, coordination, and gait control.

Not to negate ginger ale and the soothing taste of the ginger teas, but no reliefs from my dizziness occurred. Frustrated, I made an appointment to see a specialist—a professional in the ear, nose, and throat (ENT) clinic—thinking, *At last I will get some medical advice and pills to help stop this terrible feeling of dizziness and loss of balance.* As I sat waiting in this tiny room with the door closed waiting to see the doctor, I thought to myself and wondered why the door was always closed while patients sat in in an enclosed room, waiting to see the doctor, for up to thirty to thirty-five minutes? Patient privacy—I knew! But I always felt locked in and claustrophobic. I quickly opened the door slightly.

Vertigo and Loss of Balance

The cause of vertigo and a loss of balance is primarily due to the dislodging of tiny calcium crystals referred to as Ca+ particles, rocks, calcites, calcium carbonate, calcium phosphate plaques, and cholesterol particles located in the middle ear in which these crystals become dislodged, causing loss of balance and vertigo.

These *crystals* help make you sensitive to gravity and help you to keep your balance when they stay where they belong. Normally, a jelly-like membrane in our ear keeps the crystals where they belong.

Structures of the inner ear are graphically presented in the following pages to demonstrate the highly complex middle ear structure and the challenges understanding the intricate anatomy and functions the structures play.

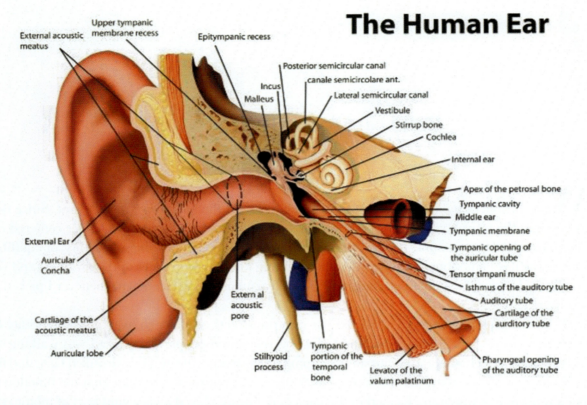

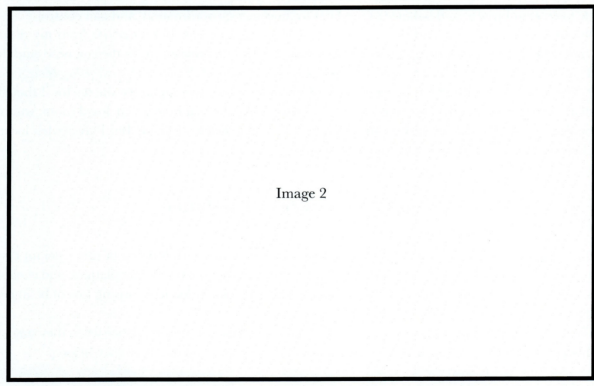

Image 2

Middle Ear Structure

Your *semicircular canals* are three tiny fluid-filled tubes in your inner ear that help you keep your balance. When your head moves around, the liquid inside the semicircular canals sloshes around and moves the tiny hairs that line each canal.

Vertigo/Dizziness

This is thought to occur because calcium carbonate crystals or "ear rocks" or *otoconia* become loose and move into one of the semicircular canals, usually the posterior portion of the semicircular canal, thereby irritating the nerve endings, which causes dizziness (see the middle ear structure above). This is a medical term referred to as benign paroxysmal positional vertigo (BPPV).

Treatment

Most people (85 percent) recover from BPPV with a neck maneuver performed by a physical therapist designed to move the crystals back where they belong into the *utricle*. The most common procedure is referred to as the *Epley maneuver*, which involves moving the head through a series of four positions and remaining in position for about thirty to sixty seconds. If after a few days the dizziness still persists, the procedure may need to be repeated several more times. Sometimes the crystals get stuck and do not move as quickly as they should, at which time a vibrating device may be used to loosen the crystals and get them to move to where they belong.

The anatomy and physiology of the inner and middle ear are, without a doubt, the most complex structures and perhaps the most difficult to comprehend, even for me as a health professional professor who has taught anatomy and physiology for years.

CHAPTER 13

Teaching Strategies for Hearing-Loss Professors

Hearing-loss professors in America and around the world are continually searching for strategies to help them teach, augment, and challenge student learning. After accepting the fact that I had lost much of my hearing and could no longer hear students in any large classroom setting and that the sound of my voice was "coming through my ears", I devised a strategy by walking up close to each student as he or she spoke. I found that I could hear and understand their questions better using this approach. Oh! What a joy it was to understand and hear what the students were saying.

If you recall, during the early phase of my hearing loss, I described a plan where I instructed students to write their comments or questions on a piece of paper and that at the end of a class session to pass their questions to the front of the class and that I would post answers to each of their questions on the blackboard. Needless to say, that was not an ideal strategy; student evaluations at the end of the course were brutal, to say the least, and I was haunted by their negative comments for a long time. I vowed then to search and to find coping strategies to assist me and other professors hard of hearing to cope. Subsequently, I located a hearing-loss teacher's dos and don'ts teaching strategies on the web.

On the first day of class, it is imperative that the teacher informs the class that he or she is hard of hearing and that he or she will need their help in order to ensure positive student learning outcomes throughout the course.

Introductions to Class

At the first class meeting, after teacher and student introductions, I began by stating that I am a hard of hearing professor and that in order to ensure the success of the class and positive learning outcomes, I was obligated to inform every class of my hearing loss situation and that I wished to share with them the teaching guidelines I would use to maximize my potentials as a professor while reinforcing their learning outcomes. After reading a copy of the guidelines, students were asked to sign a form to indicate that they understood the guidelines.

Review of Teaching Strategy—Handouts (Dos and Don'ts)

Laugh with me but not at me. Often it is comical when I misunderstand what someone is trying to say, and it is important for all of us to keep a sense of humor.

1.   Often I can tell that a student is speaking but I cannot make out all the words that he/she is saying.

2. Speak a bit more slowly than you normally do. Pronounce each word clearly. Speak more loudly than you normally do, but please do not shout. Shouting causes you to speak less clearly and will not help. Do not speak out of turn. Extra background noise will make it impossible for me to hear the speaker.

3. Raise your hand and wait to be acknowledged before speaking. If I have not called on you directly, I may not be aware that you are trying to participate.

4. Do not assume that I have heard you unless I have directly acknowledged you. This is especially true at the start of class before everyone has settled down.

5. Please be patient with me. Most people become frustrated when talking with someone who is hard of hearing and give up. But many times, the misunderstanding is very frustrating and confusing. Be aware of the difference between the two situations and do not make fun of me when it is obvious that I am struggling to understand something.

Classroom Arrangements

1. Soft-spoken students will sit near the front of the room closer to the instructor.
2. I will walk up and down the aisle to be closer to the student to hear you better.
3. I will ask a student who can hear well to sit at the front of the classroom and interpret for me if I don't understand what a student is saying.
4. I will ask a student I cannot understand to come up and write key words on the black or whiteboard.
5. I will distribute a sheet at the beginning of class that explains my hearing loss.

Assistive Devices for Hearing-Impaired Teachers

As I reflect back to the beginning of my loss of hearing, perhaps the most challenging aspect of my voyage was my search for any type of electronic device that I could find to plug into my hearing aid that would pick up the voice of the student. I spoke with the information technology person at the university who recommended the Logitech H390; I was excited until further search indicated that the headset was best suited only for online educators.

My search for electronic assistive device for hearing-loss teachers proved overwhelming and a mentally exhausting challenge. It was not until I was laid off as a

As I continued searching for assistive devices to help me hear, I located a couple of devices for hard of hearing teachers, such as the following:

1. *Pocket talker*—described as a superdirectional microphone plugged into the *pocket talker* "designed to hear the students better" and is most useful with your hearing aid to plug into a *neck loop* instead of earbuds.

2. *Voice tracker*—a devise designed to pick up student voices "anywhere in the classroom."

3. *Comfort Contego FM system*—coupled with FM transmitter and FM receiver, "allows the teacher to move freely around the classroom and still hear the student."

4. *SuperEar—YouTube.* SE 5000 / Super Personal Sound Amplifier—"This lightweight device assists those who need a little help listening to the world around them. The SuperEar® can be used to enjoy family conversations and doctor's appointments, listening to birds, music, and television."

While I invested in several of the abovementioned devices, I found that none of the ones I purchased proved very useful. This is not to say that a particular device will not serve you personally to aid you to hear students better. You are encouraged to visit various vendors specializing in solutions for all levels of hearing loss and you be the judge.

Chapter 14

Help Paying for Hearing Aid Devices

Medicare does not cover hearing exams, hearing aids, or exams for fitting hearing aids. Medicare Part B (medical insurance) covers diagnostic hearing and balance exams if your doctor or other health care provider orders them to see if you need medical treatment. If you are a federal employee or retiree, hearing aid coverage may be available through some insurance plans in the Federal Employees Health Benefits Program. Or if you are a veteran, the VA provides free hearing aids if you meet certain conditions such as being compensated for any service-connected disability or if you're hearing loss is connected to military service.

Hearing Aid Prices

Hearing aids typically range from $1,500 to $3,500 per unit. Double that if you need one for each ear! To the average American household, this is equivalent of up to two months of income. Medicare will cover hearing aids in some states for people with limited means. County social service offices have information. Millions of low-income Americans with loss of hearing cannot afford hearing aids. While there are no simple solutions there are a variety of options to explore.

Financial Assistance

Depending on your income level, there are various programs and foundations that provide financial assistance for hearing devices to people in need throughout the US; start by calling your state rehabilitation department (see www.parac.org/svrp.html). A wealth of programs include the following organizations and financial assistance units:

Lions Affordable Hearing Aid Project: Offered through some Lions Clubs throughout the US, this program provides the opportunity to purchase new digital hearing aids manufactured by Renton for $200 per aid, plus shipping. To be eligible, most clubs will require your income to be somewhere below 200 percent of the federal poverty level, which is $22,340 for singles or $30,260 for couples. Contact your local Lions club to see if they participate in this project.

Seroma: A civic service organization that runs a hearing aid recycling program through its five hundred clubs nationwide, refurbishes them, and distributes them to local people in need. Call 800-593-5646 or visit sertoma.org to locate a club in your area.

Audient: This program (audientalliance.org, 866-956-5400) helps people purchase new digital hearing aids at reduced prices, ranging from $495 to $975 for one hearing aid or $990 to $1,575 for a pair. To be eligible, your income must be below $27,075 for singles or $36,425 for couples annually.

Hope for Hearing (Donated Hearing Aids)

Comprehensive audiology care, including donated hearing aids (refurbished), is being provided to indigent patients in free clinics and major academic centers.

Ear Community

Ear Community is a charitable organization that helps individuals who were born with microbial and atresia. If you need help obtaining a BAHA (bone conduction hearing device) and have been denied by your insurance plan or cannot afford to purchase https://earcommunity.org/donate/application-for-a-bone-conductive-hearing-device/

Starkey Hearing Foundation and Hear Now

Assistance for low-income individuals permanently residing in the US with no other resources to acquire hearing aids

6700 Washington Avenue South
Eden Prairie, MN 55344
Ph.: 800-328-8602 (voice-ask for Hear Now)
(952) 947-4997 Fax
www.starkeyhearingfoundation.org
http://www.sotheworldmayhear.org

Cochlear Americas Scholarships

Customer service financial support line
For help with insurance appeals through
Ph.: 1-800-633-4667
(The scholarships are available internationally.)

AG Bell Financial Grant

The child must be three (3) years old or younger as of December 31, 20xx. Child must have a documented bilateral hearing loss, and this grant is only for children with a bilateral hearing loss and is unfortunately not open to unilateral hearing-loss children. http://nc.agbell.org/netcommunity/page.aspx?pid=499&srctid=1&erid=1730670&trid=25f

UnitedHealthcare Children's Foundation

Will cover up to $5,000 in uncovered medical costs per year for people with private (not public) insurance (for hearing loss)

www.uhccf.org

The Better Hearing Organization

This document takes a while to load but is absolutely worth it. It is loaded with organizations who offer financial assistance programs for obtaining hearing aids.

www.betterhearing.org

Black Hearing-Impaired Students Scholarship

In partnership with Gallaudet University, this scholarship is intended for Black deaf and hard of hearing students of Gallaudet University who demonstrate financial need with a GPA of 3.0 or better. The university maintains the funds and the application process.

Preference is given to those who demonstrate a desire to advance the lives of Black deaf and hard of hearing people. To donate to this fund, please access Gallaudet University's giving page. Instructions: select "Other" when you click on the "Giving On-Line" box. In the Other box, type "Andrew Foster Scholarship."

Children's Hospitals around the World

Contact a children's hospital closest to you and ask about their scholarship program. Apparently, many children's hospitals offer financial assistance through a scholarship that you can apply for that can help you with a 35 percent discount toward the purchase or insurance coverage for an assisted hearing device. Income is taken into account, and you must make no more than a combined income of $80,000 annually in order to qualify.

Better Hearing Institute

Financial Assistance Guide
1444 I Street, NW, Suite 700
Washington, DC 20005
(202) 449-1100 Voice

(202) 216-9646 Fax
1-800-EAR-WELL

Equality Scholarship

- Application deadline: 1/31/2020
- Amount: $6,000
- eQuality Scholarship Collaborative awards scholarships to honor and encourage California students for their service to the lesbian/gay/bisexual/transgender community. Applicants for all scholarships must have demonstrated service to the LGBT+ community. Applicants of all sexual orientations and gender identities are eligible.

Pride Foundation Scholarships

- Application deadline: 1/12/2020
- Amount: $10,000
- The Pride Foundation offers more than fifty different scholarships though there is only one application to complete. Scholarships are available to lesbian, gay, bisexual, transgender, queer, and straight-ally (straight and supportive of LGBT issues) students as well as students from LGBT families. Students must either be residents of Alaska, Idaho, Montana, Oregon, or Washington (but may study [...] More

Children of the Silent World

Assists low-income children with purchasing hearing aids
PO Box 2425
Cridersville, OH 45806

Disabled Children's Relief Fund

Provides assistance to families of children with disabilities, with preference for children with physical disabilities and little or no health insurance
PO Box 89
Freeport, New York 11520
(516) 377-1605 Voice
(516) 377-3978 Fax
http://www.dcrf.com/

Easter Seals

Over four hundred local service centers with varying services; some assist low-income adults and children with hearing aids and other rehabilitative devices.

230 West Monroe Street, Suite 1800 Chicago, IL 60606

Gates Millennium Scholars Program

Scholarships for African American, American Indian / Alaska Native, Asian Pacific Islander American, and Hispanic American students with high academic and leadership promise who have significant financial need and an interest in the disciplines of computer science, education, engineering, library science, mathematics, public health and the sciences, where these groups are severely underrepresented.

Generation Google Scholarship

Helps minority students who plan to attend college and study computer science and technology. Eligible students must be African American, Hispanic, American Indian, and Filipino / Native Hawaiian / Pacific Islander.

Hispanic Scholarship Fund

The Hispanic Scholarship Fund (HSF) is the nation's leading organization supporting Hispanic higher education. Scholarships are available at this site for community college transfer students.

NAACP Scholarships

Provides scholarships for NAACP members currently enrolled or accepted to an accredited college or university in the United States.

Ron Brown Scholarship

Recipients are young African Americans of outstanding promise who are offered academic scholarships, service opportunities, and leadership experiences. Scholars are each awarded $40,000 ($10,000 per year for four years toward educational expenses) that may be used at the college or university of their choice.

United Negro College Fund

Provides extraordinary amounts of scholarship opportunities for minority students with financial need. UNCF is the nation's largest private scholarship provider to minority group members. Each year, more than $100 million in scholarships are awarded to more than ten thousand students at more than 1,100 schools across the country.

CaptionCall—US Government–Sponsored

A revolutionary service for people who have difficulty using the phone due to hearing loss even when using a hearing aid or enhanced amplification. Similar to captioned television but available to qualified people with hearing loss. CaptionCall transmits the hearing party's speech to a communications assistant who converts it into text.

CHAPTER 15

Opportunities to Serve as Volunteers

The personal fulfillment and satisfaction of volunteering can instill a sense of gaining new experiences, helping others and giving back, connecting with people and cultures, a sense of purpose and emotional satisfaction, as well as exploring future career option.

Anyone can apply to become a volunteer. You may have a hearing loss yourself or be a partner of someone with a hearing loss or just want to help those who have a hearing loss. There are many opportunities for volunteers and interns working with service projects, planning and staffing events, to grant writing, and photography.

There are literally thousands of opportunities to serve as a volunteer for the deaf and hard of hearing in America and abroad. Websites include a wealth of services available to those who wish to volunteer to work with children or adults, companion for seniors, working with the deaf in India, Abused Deaf Women's Advocacy Service, Deaf Reach walks in the community, volunteering to help the deaf and hearing-loss people communicate with their doctors, income tax assistant for the hearing-impaired, volunteer opportunities at the Smithsonian Art Museum, and teaching in Cape Town, South Africa.

In my search, I discovered an inspiring story of a young man, deaf since a young age, who sat out to find a place so far removed that his deafness would become irrelevant. The place turned out to be Zambia in a remote African village where he worked as a Peace Corps volunteer, working in a health clinic, a place where he believed his deafness didn't interfere, a place where he felt at home despite his encounter with "night marsh incidents and gripping narratives." Read the story as told by Josh Swiller (2007) in the book *The Unheard.*

Deaf Education Volunteer Projects—empowers deaf communities by increasing education, literacy, job skills, and economic self-sufficiency

Jamaica

Deaf and Hard of Hearing Programs Abroad-Jamaica Volunteers—"If you are a sign language interpreter or student, come to Jamaica for deaf and hard of hearing programs and help to empower the deaf community."

The Hearing and Speech Foundation—"Raising money to support a nonprofit organization is a lot of work and would not be possible without the support of community volunteers. Thanks to our hearing aid recycling program, we are able to off-set the cost of hearing aids to our clients."

Volunteers / Deaf Volunteers —Oversees volunteering with your family is an excellent way to a more meaningful holiday experience. You will work together at a deaf school doing practical work, arts and crafts, and playing educational games with local students while learning about a new culture.

Philippines

Volunteer at School for Deaf Children in the Philippines—Bring your sign at a school for deaf children. You will work with the children and teachers.

Deaf International Exchange Opportunities—Exchange program providers and universities have worked with many participants to arrange sign language interpreters abroad, real-time captioning. Ashanti School for the Deaf (Ghana), the school for the deaf looks for volunteers to be teacher assistants in their classrooms.

"10 Deaf Friendly Ways to Travel the World Cheaply"—Deaf and hearing Peace Corps volunteers in Bulgaria, Guyana, Jamaica, and Kenya and use sign language to conduct classes in science and social studies.

Teaching Deaf People in Nepal—Would you like to be a deaf volunteer in Nepal? Then your time to volunteer to teach the deaf people has arrived. Maybe you know sign language, have a deaf family member, or have experienced working or teaching in a deaf community or you yourself are hearing-impaired.

CHAPTER 16

Communicating with People with Hearing Loss

One of the most stressful situations as a hearing-loss person is when family members and others, when I attempt to communicate and I tell them, "I cannot hear you," they become annoyed or refuse to repeat what they've said by saying, "Never mind!"

Successful communication requires the efforts of all people involved in a conversation. Even when the person with hearing loss utilizes hearing aids and active listening strategies, it is crucial that others involved in the communication process consistently use good communication practices, including the following:

1. *Face the nonhearing person directly—on the same level and in good light whenever possible.* Position yourself so that the light is shining on the speaker's face, not in the eyes of the listener.

2. *Do not talk from another room.* Not being able to see each other when talking is a common reason people have difficulty understanding what is said.

3. *Speak clearly, slowly, distinctly, but naturally, without shouting or exaggerating mouth movements.* Shouting distorts the sound of speech and may make speech reading more difficult.

4. *Say the person's name before beginning a conversation.* This gives the listener a chance to focus attention and reduces the chance of missing words at the beginning of the conversation.

5. *Avoid talking too rapidly or using sentences that are too complex.* Slow down a little, pause between sentences or phrases, and wait to make sure you have been understood before going on.

6. *Keep your hands away from your face while talking.* If you are eating, chewing, smoking, etc. while talking, your speech will be more difficult to understand. Beards and moustaches can also interfere with the ability of the hearing-impaired to understand speech.

7. If the hearing-impaired listener hears better in one ear than the other, try to make a point of remembering which ear is better so that you will *know where to position yourself.*

8. *Be aware of possible distortion of sounds for the hearing-impaired person.* They may hear your voice but still may have difficulty understanding words. Most hearing-loss people have greater difficulty understanding speech when there is background noise. Some people with hearing loss are very sensitive to loud sounds. Tolerance for loud sounds is not uncommon. Avoid situations where there will be loud sounds when possible.

9. If the hearing-loss person has difficulty understanding a particular phrase or word, *try to find a different way of saying the same thing* rather than repeating the original words over and over.

10. *Acquaint the listener with the general topic of the conversation.* Avoid sudden changes of topic. If the subject is changed, tell the hearing-impaired person what you are talking about now. In a group setting, repeat questions or key facts before continuing with the discussion. If you are giving specific

information—such as time, place, or phone numbers—to someone who is hearing-impaired, have them repeat the specifics back to you. Many numbers and words sound alike.

11. *Provide pertinent information in writing*, such as directions, schedules, and work assignments.

12. Recognize that everyone, especially the hard of hearing, has a harder time hearing and understanding *when ill or tired.*

13. *Pay attention to the listener.* A puzzled look may indicate misunderstanding. Tactfully ask the person if they understood you.

CHAPTER 17

A Proposed Center for the Hearing Loss and Deaf Culture

I hereby propose that every teaching-learning institution in America and around the world commit to undertaking a "Hearing Loss and Deaf Culture Center for the Hearing-Impaired Teachers, Students, and the Community." And that such a center be funded as part of the institution's annual budget and/or through the expansion of governmental grants developed by the institution's research and development officers.

Mission Statement

To empower deaf cultures and hard of hearing individuals to live independently and productively within American society and around the world.

The center would develop flyers and have copies available for its community constituents, faculty, students, and anyone who is interested, particularly parties who wish to further and/or contribute to the mission and objectives of the center.

The term "deaf" generally refers to people who were born without the ability to hear. Individuals who are deaf may have little or no speech depending on the severity of the hearing loss and the age of onset. They will often communicate through a sign language or an interpreter and prefers the term "deaf culture" as oppose to "hearing-impaired."

How to Live Comfortably with Deafness

The aim, thus, is to encourage people who are deaf to use American Sign Language (ASL). It has its own grammar and word order. Other students may use manual English (or signed English), which is sign language in English word order. A certified interpreter is used for translation into either language. Students who are deaf may also benefit from real-time captioning, where spoken text is typed and projected onto a screen.

Hard of Hearing

"Hard of hearing" refers to the slow progression of hearing loss. Some students who are hard of hearing may hear only specific frequencies or sounds within a certain volume range. They may have speech impairments because of their inability to hear their own voices clearly. These students may rely heavily on hearing aids and lipreading. Some students who are hard of hearing may never learn sign language.

People who are hard of hearing may find it difficult to simultaneously watch demonstrations and follow verbal descriptions, especially if they are watching a sign language interpreter, a captioning screen, or a speaker's lips. Small group discussions may also be difficult to follow or participate in, particularly if the discussion is fast-paced and unmoderated since there is often lag time between a speaker's comments and interpretation.

As a hard of hearing person, I often cannot understand what a person is saying. Or occasionally, it sounds like everyone is mumbling and they don't speak clearly—particularly, individuals who speak with an accent. I have a more difficult time hearing the high-pitched consonant sounds (such as *d, t, she, s, f, the*) compared to the lower-pitched vowel sounds (such as *o, a, ah, I, e*).

Living Comfortably Being Hard of Hearing (although Difficult)

If hearing aids are used, the person will likely benefit from amplification in other forms, such as assistive listening devices (ALDs) like hearing aid compatible telephones, personal neck loops, and audio induction loop assistive listening systems. Some students use FM amplification systems that require the presenter to wear a small microphone to transmit amplification.

Services Offered through the Hard of Hearing Center

Being deaf or hard of hearing can affect students in many ways. They may have difficulty following lectures, particularly if the acoustics causes echoes or if the speaker talks softly, fast, or unclearly. However, with the help from our staff at the *Deaf and Hard of Hearing Center*, the quality of life of those who are hard of hearing will increase.

A list of aids available at our Deaf and Hard of Hearing Center will include interpreters, sound amplification systems, notetakers, real-time captioning, email for faculty-student meetings and class discussions, visual warning systems for lab emergencies, changing computer auditory signals to flash changes, captioned video presentations, sign language, lipreading, and electronic hearing devices.

2ND TO 8TH
MAY 2016

COMMON PURPOSE

SIX MISSION GROUPS WILL DEVELOP A COLLABORATIVE PROGRAMME OF WORK. THEY ARE:

- AWARENESS
- INFORMATION
- EDUCATION
- SERVICES
- EMPLOYMENT
- PREVENTION

WWW.DEAFCOUNCIL.ORG.UK/ABOUT-US/COMMON-PURPOSE

DEAFNESS - SOME FACTS

- 1 IN 6 PEOPLE IN THE UK ARE AFFECTED BY HEARING LOSS (@ 10 MILLION)
- 6.5 MILLION OF THESE ARE AGED 60 AND OVER
- 3.7 MILLION ARE OF WORKING AGE
- AROUND 2 MILLION PEOPLE IN THE UK HAVE HEARING AIDS
- ABOUT 800,000 ARE SEVERELY OR PROFOUNDLY DEAF
- ADULTS AND CHILDREN WHO ARE DEAF OR HARD OF HEARING FACE COMMUNICATION BARRIERS WHICH CAN CAUSE:
  - LACK OF CONFIDENCE
  - ISOLATION
  - EXCLUSION FROM SOCIETY
  - UNEMPLOYMENT
  - DEPRESSION
- TECHNOLOGY AND THE WAY WE COMMUNICATE IS HELPING TO CHANGE THIS

DEAF AWARENESS WEEK

Deaf Awareness Week is co-ordinated by the UK Council on Deafness

Registered Charity No. 1038448
www.deafcouncil.org.uk

CHAPTER 18

Family Suicides and Diagnosis of Kidney Disease

I received a call from my sister Carolyn informing me that our mother who had been ill had been diagnosed with colon cancer and was being transferred to a hospice facility waiting to die. I immediately boarded a plane from Chicago to Houston to be with her.

As I entered my mom's room, she was in a coma and quietly breathing. My sister Betty placed her arms around me and softly said, "She's been waiting for you to come home."

I began to cry and whispered, "It's okay for you to go, Mama. It's okay for you to go, Mama." Within the hour, she took her last breath and was gone. I knelt down holding her hand, quietly crying.

Both my father and my brother committed suicide. They each took a gun, placed it against their temples, and blew their brains out. At the time, I was devastated. I painfully mourned the deaths of my father and my brother and wondered what in their lives drove them to end their existence on this earth in such a violent manner, leaving behind so much pain in the hearts of their loved ones.

Death is a challenge. It tells us not to waste time …
It tells us to tell each other right now that we love each other.

Kidney Disease

As I faced yet another day down the road of life's uncertainty waiting for Godot, I would take daily walks routinely for about eight to ten blocks. One day I suddenly felt a terrible sense of feeling faint and weak. With all the strength I could muster, I continued to walk and stopped at a nearby Starbucks to rest and gather my momentum. Once the dizziness and weakness subsided, I continued my walk back home and pondered why this awful episode had occurred.

Throughout that particular summer, I continued to experience severe generalized weakness and severe muscle cramps in my legs and my hands; so much so that it literally reduced me to tears.

I was urinating three to four times during the night. There was no swelling in my ankles or my feet, so I ignored these symptoms and passed it off as due to the aging process. As the weakness persisted and I could no longer walk two to three blocks, I made an appointment in to see my internist; and at the time, he ordered a series of blood test, EKG, and chest x-rays. He also indicated that my blood pressure was too high (190/90) and gave me a prescription to bring the blood pressure down.

Prior to my return appointment to see the internist, I literally felt so sick and weak, I could hardly walk a block. In my follow-up appointment, the internist informed me that all the diagnostic tests were in and that my blood test indicated the probable cause of my symptoms. As he peered at his computer screen, he cautiously looked at me and said, "You have stage 4 kidney disease. Your glomeruli filtration rate is not within the normal rate."

I felt utterly devastated and wondered how long this kidney disease had been in progress and just how long I could live with both a loss of hearing (deafness) and a chronic kidney problem? Surely my days on this earth were numbered.

There are more than thirty million American adults living with a kidney disease, and most don't know it. There are a number of physical signs of kidney disease, but sometimes people attribute them to other conditions. Also, those with kidney disease tend not to experience symptoms until the very late stages, when the kidneys are failing or when there are large amounts of protein in the urine.

Chronic Kidney Disease

Chronic kidney disease (CKD) is divided into five stages based on the level of kidney function. Stages are determined through certain tests performed by your doctor, including a test used to calculate estimated glomerular filtration rate (eGFR), which measures how well your kidneys are cleaning your blood.

Kidney disease is a progressive disease, meaning that kidney function can continue to decline over time, eventually resulting in kidney failure. The internist indicated that my glomerular filtration rate was identified at being at Stage 4-GFR 29-15) / GFR of 29-15, indicating severe loss of kidney function.

In my mind's eye, I visualized the inner working of my kidneys: the nephrons and the glomeruli, as blood and urine flow through these hundreds of tiny microscopic cellular structures inside, the kidneys used to cleanse my blood of toxins and waste and out the body through the urine. I also knew that the kidneys produced a hormone needed to make red blood cells.

To be precise, each *kidney* is made up of about a million filtering units called *nephrons*. Each nephron includes a filter called the glomerulus and a tubule. Nephrons work through a two-step process: the glomerulus filters your blood and the tubule returns needed substances to your blood and removes wastes (sounds complex? It is).

Kidney disease is categorized in stages by its ability to filter out waste from the blood (i.e., stages 1 through 5 [stage 4 = severe loss of kidney function and stage 5 resulting in total kidney failure necessitating the need to undergo dialysis in order to survive]).

Signs You May Have Kidney Disease

You're more tired, have less energy, or are having trouble concentrating. A severe decrease in kidney function can lead to a buildup of toxins and impurities in the blood. This can cause people to feel tired and weak and can make it hard to concentrate. Another complication of kidney disease is anemia, which can cause weakness and fatigue.

You're having trouble sleeping. When the kidneys aren't filtering properly, toxins stay in the blood rather than leave the body through the urine.

You have dry and itchy skin. Healthy kidneys do many important jobs. They remove wastes and extra fluid from your body, help make red blood cells, help keep bones strong, and work to maintain the right amount of minerals in your blood. Dry and itchy skin can be a sign of the mineral and bone disease that often accompanies advanced kidney disease.

You feel the need to urinate more often. If you feel the need to urinate more often, especially at night, this can be a sign of kidney disease. When the kidneys' filters are damaged, it can cause an increase in the urge to urinate.

You see blood in your urine. Healthy kidneys typically keep the blood cells in the body when filtering wastes from the blood to create urine, but when the kidneys' filters have been damaged, these blood cells can start to leak out into the urine.

Your urine is foamy. Excessive bubbles in the urine—especially those that require you to flush several times before they go away—indicate protein in the urine. This foam may look like the foam you see when scrambling eggs, as the common protein found in urine, albumin, is the same protein that is found in eggs.

You're experiencing persistent puffiness around your eyes. Protein in the urine is an early sign that the kidneys' filters have been damaged, allowing protein to leak into the urine. This puffiness around your eyes can be due to the fact that your kidneys are leaking a large amount of protein in the urine rather than keeping it in the body.

Your ankles and feet are swollen. Decreased kidney function can lead to sodium retention, causing swelling in your feet and ankles.

You have a poor appetite. This is a very general symptom, but a buildup of toxins resulting from reduced kidney function can be one of the causes.

Your muscles are cramping. Electrolyte imbalances can result from impaired kidney function. For example, low calcium levels and poorly controlled phosphorus may contribute to muscle cramping.

I've learned a lot about a lot of things and yet not enough about other things—particularly, about *omens* and forewarnings of death.

Um Aprendo

AFTERWORD

I received a call from my sister Carolyn, that our mother who was in the hospital
Was now in a hospice facility to await her death. I immediately boarded a plane
from Chicago to Houston to be with mama and the family. Upon my arrival, as I sat next
to her bed, she lay quietly in a coma. I called out to her "Oh Mama! It's, okay you can
Go now mama" I sat there, held her hand and sobbed quietly.
Both my father and my brother had committed suicide. They each took a gun
Placed it against their temples and blew their brains out. At the time, I wondered what
Could have been so painful, that each had choose to end their lives. What had caused
My loved ones to committee suicide? I could not imagine anything worse than the pain I felt when I
lost both my parents to such a heartbreaking stage in my life.

My brother and I were just nine months apart. A week before my brother took a gun, held it to his
temple, and committed suicide, at around 11:00 a.m., in the middle of the city in Denver, Colorado, as I
headed out to teach a class, there suddenly appeared perched atop the railing high above the garage door
a white, brownish spotted owl. It appeared not to be startled by my presence and never once moved from
its perch high above the garage door. As I proceeded to my car and drove a distance, I stopped the car and
looked back toward the garage. The owl continued to sit perched high atop the garage door.

A week later, early in the morning, my phone rang, and it was my sister Debra from California. She was
hysterical and crying out loud, "Sidney just killed himself. Sidney killed himself." She continued sobbing
and screaming at the top of her voice. I, too, began crying and repeating out loud, "Why? Oh, God, why?"
Between the pain and suffering I could hear in my sister's voice, I heard her say quietly, "I'll call you back"
and hung up the phone.

In the back of my mind, I suddenly envisioned a picture of the white owl I saw perched high above the
ledge on my garage door, and I wondered if the myths surrounding the white owl were true:

The Legend of the White Owl

People have associated owls with wisdom since before recorded history. This belief evolved separately in
several different cultures. Owls, as night birds, are shrouded in mystery and are apt to become depositories
for superstitions, just as nightjars and bats have. Most of the original beliefs linked owls to evil. Over time,
the beliefs evolved, and it became a teller of death, a bringer of ill omens, and a bird of prophecy.

Owls Are a Sign of Death in Many Cultures

For instance, dreaming of an owl signified approaching death for Apache people. Boreal owl calls were a call from spirits to the Cree people, and if you answered back to the owl with a whistle and didn't get a response, it was a sign that your death was imminent. On the other hand, Dakota Hidatsa people believed that burrowing owls acted as protective spirits for warriors, so not all owls were bad.

The Moan Bird

According to myth, an owl sat on Athena's blind side so that she could see the whole truth. In Ancient Greece, the owl was a symbol of a higher wisdom, and it was also a guardian of the Acropolis. The Mayans called the screech owl of the Yucatan the moan bird and believed that it meant *death*.

For Some Cultures, the Owl Is Sacred

Among Aboriginal Australian, owls are the spirits of women and so are sacred. The Kwakiutl people also thought owls were the souls of people and shouldn't be harmed because if an owl was killed, the person whose soul the owl carried would also die. In fact, many different cultures believed that a person became an owl after death. It is also said that people born between November 23 and December 21 are "wise and filled with higher wisdom." I support the legend, for I was born on December 7.

My brother's funeral was sad and mournful; it brought together the love and togetherness of our family. And yet while my brother served in the navy, I cannot recall if military honors, such as taps or folding of the flag, were a part of the ceremony. My memories at the grave site are blurred and almost erased from my mind although I try so hard to remember.

My mind tends to wander back to the times when we were children raised in the country on the dairy. Oh! What beautiful memories … I wish that I could relive those moments just one more time.

Grazie—Italian
Dance dir—German
Merci—French
Dziekuye—Polish
Bol' shoy spasibo—Russian
Thank you—American

INDEX

ABOUT THE AUTHOR

Developed and Lecturer for newly developed course: Master of Science in Nursing (MSN) entitled: Ethics, Health Policy, and Finance. Team taught with my lectures focusing on "Health Policy and Nursing."

Courses taught included: (1) Fundamentals of Nursing, encompassing, both lectures and supervision of students in hospital setting, at a major Chicago area hospital weekly, from 6:00AM-4:00PM. Public Health/Community Health Nursing (didactic and clinical); (3) Essentials of Leadership in Nursing and (4) Introduction to Health Professions.

- Taught students basic-fundamental principles and concepts of nursing care for sick and infirmed clients.
- Supervised student nurse interns at major medical center, caring for patients with medical and/or surgical health care needs.
- Work shop on "Electronic Medical Records" (mandatory) for both professors and student interns attended prior to clinical affiliation.
- Developed state of the art power point lecture series for Fundamental of Nursing lectures.
- Successfully correlated didactic teachings to care of patients in both acute and chronic patient care situations.
- Implemented Critical Thinking Model for student use; to grasp logic and understanding of reading and writing assignments across nursing nurses.
- Master of Science in Nursing (Nursing 5145): Ethics, Health Policy and Finance in Nursing" – A series of power point lectures, developed for Health Policy and Nursing.
- Developed Model for MSN course entitled: Logic and Critical Thinking Applied to the Study of Health Policy and Nursing; Model presented at CSU's –" Faculty Festival" via The Center for Research and Faculty Development.
- Lead teacher and course coordinator for Leadership in Nursing Course.
- Leadership and Management –Classical power points series developed for selected course content areas.
- Implemented a variety of contemporary teaching strategies in courses: Introduction to Health Professions and Community Health Nursing: s i.e. Debates, Photo Journaling (visual Arts), Acting (Performing Arts,) Cartooning and graphics depictions.
- Conducted preliminary "Data Collection" for research study entitled: Assessment of Student Learning Styles in Introductory Health professions Course."

Other courses taught included: (2) Public Health/Community Health Nursing (didactic and clinical); (3) Essentials of Leadership in Nursing and (4) Introduction to Health Professions.

- Taught students basic-fundamental principles and concepts of nursing care for sick and infirmed clients.
- Supervised student nurse interns at major medical center, caring for patients with medical and/or surgical health care needs.

- Work shop on "Electronic Medical Records" (mandatory) for both professors and student interns attended prior to clinical affiliation.
- Developed state of the art power point lecture series for Fundamental of Nursing lectures.
- Successfully correlated didactic teachings to care of patients in both acute and chronic patient care situations.
- Implemented Critical Thinking Model for student use; to grasp logic and understanding of reading and writing assignments across nursing nurses.
- Master of Science in Nursing (Nursing 5145): Ethics, Health Policy and Finance in Nursing" – A series of power point lectures, developed for Health Policy and Nursing.
- Developed Model for MSN course entitled: Logic and Critical Thinking Applied to the Study of Health Policy and Nursing; Model presented at CSU's –" Faculty Festival" via The Center for Research and Faculty Development.
- Lead teacher and course coordinator for Leadership in Nursing Course.
- Leadership and Management –Classical power points series developed for selected course content areas.
- Secured the Executive Director of the Illinois Nurses Association (Ms. Susan Swart), to serve as speaker to the Leadership and Nursing class at Chicago State University.
- Implemented a variety of contemporary teaching strategies in courses: Introduction to Health Professions and Community Health Nursing: s i.e. Debates, Photo Journaling (visual Arts), Acting (Performing Arts,) Cartooning and graphics depictions.
- Conducted preliminary "Data Collection" for research study entitled: Assessment of Student Learning Styles in Introductory Health professions Course."